THE KING SAUL SPIRIT

A Demonic Force of Destruction
That Has To Be Stopped

By
Hansie Steyn

Dear Roman,

Be blessed bo.

God loves you and
you are a great man of
God.

Is 1:19

Laurie

May 09

CONTENTS

—◊◊◊—

INTRODUCTION

—〜〜—

After my military training in 1972, I went to university and studied to become a teacher. During my teaching career, I started singing and playing in rock bands. Eventually, I became a full-time rock singer in nightclubs. Then my life turned around one day, and I got saved on November the 4th, 1983. I had been to the nightclub the Saturday night before and woke up Sunday morning feeling awful. That's when I heard an audible voice telling me to go to church. Well, when you hear things like that, you do what it says. In church I was bored and just sat there waiting for it to finish. All of a sudden they were taking communion. I did not know what it was, but when the preacher said you could only partake if you were born-again I realized I did not know Jesus. Before I could stop myself I was walking down the aisle to the front where I gave my life to the Lord. What a great day in my life that was! I had no Christian background and had to learn quickly, because I wanted to work for God. I had been working full-time for the devil, but now my mind was set on working full-time for God. God set me free from my sins, Jesus came into my heart, and I knew that I was accepted by the loving almighty God Himself.

As a new born-again believer, I thought everyone I saw in church felt like me, thought like me, and was happy to be out of the demonic side of the world. To my surprise, it was not so. Not everyone lifting their hands, singing, and shouting in church was as innocent as they seemed. I was a musician and wanted to sing for the Lord. So God let me meet my precious wife, Jeanette, whose dad was a minister. He was a great man of God, and he helped me a lot in my Christian life. Jeanette and I both had a passion for music, and with her music degree, it wasn't long before we were writing our own songs and recording with a record company. God blessed me with a teaching ability, and very soon we were singing and preaching the Word of God all over South Africa. In the meantime, I had become a lecturer at a university. After a few years, God called me out of that position and into full-time ministry.

My wife, my daughter, and I have been on the road now, evangelizing and singing, for eighteen years. The three of us have toured South Africa for many years. In 2001, God told us to give up everything in South Africa and move to America. In obedience we did just that, although it was difficult leaving our home country for a new place with a different culture.

Ever since I became a Christian, but especially during our travels in South Africa and America, we saw an alarming trend in our churches. We saw precious children of God backslide, and Christians, who had been born again for many years, hurt and destroyed. We saw churches split, pastors being treated like dirt, and pastors treating church members, and even visitors like ourselves, like dirt. In my first year as a new Christian, I told my wife, *"If this is Christianity, I don't want it. Even in the world I was treated better than by some of the Christians. I thought we should love each other."* My dear precious wife, who had been a child of God since she was very young, just looked at me and said, *"I'm sorry, my babe, I don't know what to say. All I can say is this: don't look at people, they will fail you. Just keep your eyes on Jesus. Look at God; He will never fail you."* Those words, my friend, saved me from backsliding. The way the Christians were behaving almost caused me to fall. I could not understand how people with Jesus in their hearts could be so impatient, angry, deceitful, jealous, prideful, and self-willed. Many were rebellious to God's Word, as if they didn't care what it said. They went out of their way to destroy each other and their churches. I saw Christians hurt, criticize, gossip, and judge each other.

Unfortunately, I'm still seeing the same thing happen in our churches today. Nothing has changed. In South Africa, in North Africa and even in America, it's the same, all over. I don't think God wants Christians to destroy each other. It's bad enough that we have to resist the devil and his demons. We don't have to fight each other, too. There is no scripture that says we should. As a matter of fact, Jesus said we should love each other. That's when everyone will see that we are His disciples, His people, and

His children. What is so difficult to understand about this scripture?

> A new commandment I give to you, that you love one another; as I have loved you, that you also love one another. By this all will know that you are My disciples, if you have love for one another.
>
> —John 13:34-35

I'm not seeing the love that Jesus spoke about in our churches. I'm seeing too many Christians destroying other Christians and thinking nothing about it.

In South Africa and in America, even in the whole world, something is wrong. Something must be behind this destruction process. We know the enemy is out there, like a roaring lion, trying to devour and attack us, right? Why are Christians giving in to this attack? Why are we allowing the enemy to use us to attack one another? The devil's main activity is to get us mad at or offended by one another. Then it's Christian against Christian, destroying one another's lives to the extent that many of those Christians backslide and never serve God again. Some of them will tell you, "*I don't believe in God anymore. It's because of the church. Church members have hurt me too much. They're a bunch of hypocrites.*" Ever heard those words? Well, I have, many times.

Too many churches are splitting up because of infighting—church members disagreeing with and destroying one another. Too many ministers are leaving the pulpit and missing God's call on their lives. Not only are they leaving, but some are backsliding altogether. Something is wrong when Christians are being used to destroy Christians.

"Oh you're wearing a new dress again, did you use our tithe money to buy it?" Someone asked this of a precious pastor's wife, who was working and earning her own money; she was not buying her dresses using the tithe money of the church. She was using her own hard-earned income. It had nothing to do with the nosy religious lady. This lady interrogated the pastor's wife every Sunday. Guess what? The pastor's wife ended up not coming to church for three years. The pastor did not do much about the situation, because he didn't know why it was happening or how to handle it. Only when he realized what spirit was attacking his church did he ask the lady to leave and attend another church. That's when his wife was restored and made whole again. He almost lost his wife through a nagging, prideful, jealous lady, who just did not like the pastor's wife. Well then, why did she just not leave the church? Why stay and try and destroy the pastor's wife? The reason is that there is a spirit behind all of this destruction going on in our churches. The question is: what spirit? Well, that's what we're going to discuss in this book.

What about this story? I'm sure you've heard this one before. A new pastor came to a church. He was voted in 100 percent. Everyone agreed he was the right guy. Within six months, he started suggesting and making some changes. People liked this, because they wanted something new. They wanted some new music, new administration, new meetings, new carpet, and new paint colors in the church. Only a couple of religious people, maybe one or two, didn't like what the pastor was doing. Just six months ago, when he told them what he wanted to do, they voted yes. Now, it's a problem. Many times the resistance comes from a board member, a deacon, or just a member of the church.

They start giving this poor pastor such a hard time. They criticize his preaching. They speak evil behind his back. They attack his children and his wife. They accuse him of spending the church's money wrongly. They involve other people from the church and corrupt their minds as well. None of this is true, of course, but the word is out all over town. Even if someone tried covering up everything they've said, it's too late: the pastor's name is down the drain. People who voted him in now want him to resign. How about that? The same people, who said that God had given them a wonderful new pastor, all of a sudden want him to resign. What an insult to God, accusing Him of being confused. First God gives them the right guy, and then God apparently says that it's not the right guy. Come on—what a mess the church is in! I've heard these words too many times: "*God told me.*" Meanwhile, it wasn't God; God's not confused. This pastor got so hurt that he backslid, my friend. Yes, he got away from God and ended up working as an insurance broker. His calling and ministry were destroyed because of other Christians. He stopped serving God altogether. Why does this happen? I hope that, after reading this book, you'll have a greater understanding of why these things are happening in our churches, maybe even in your church. I hope we will be able to stop the destructive process of this evil demonic spirit.

I can go on and on, and you probably know more stories than I do, because it's happened in your church already. We have to get the answer somewhere, then do something about it, and stop this destruction among Christians. Please bear with me and help me to identify this evil spirit, attacking and destroying churches around the world.

God showed me what the problem was and how to solve it. He's helped me to identify the spirit we're encountering in our churches. I hope you'll enjoy the journey with me as we study and identify how to counterattack this evil demonic spirit: the King Saul spirit.

PART ONE

THE KING SAUL SPIRIT

—m—

CHAPTER 1

What Is the King Saul Spirit?

—⁓—

There has been a lot of writing on different kinds of spirits that have infiltrated our churches and attacked Christians. One of the best known is the Jezebel spirit. I am not going to go into great detail regarding who and what the Jezebel spirit is. You can go and buy some excellent books on this topic at your local Christian bookstore. However, I have to remind you what this spirit can do, and where it comes from, because this book is going to go further than the Jezebel spirit.

The Jezebel spirit is a controlling spirit. In the Bible, Jezebel controlled her husband, Ahab. She told him what to do and what not to do. That's why we talk about a person that is a Jezebel, or has a Jezebel spirit, as someone that wants to be in control of every situation and every person around them. I believe some people can even be possessed by this spirit. Usually, the Jezebel spirit attacks and oppresses people in order to direct their actions. This means that they become controllers and want to control people, husbands, wives, pastors, churches, situations, etc. When we say, *"There is a Jezebel spirit in this church,"* we mean that someone wants to control the church and the pastor, or is controlling the church and the pastor already. Usually it is good to get rid of such a person, because they will destroy the church. Sometimes it takes a while before you discern this spirit in someone's life, but when you do, it's better to ask them to leave or be delivered. Don't play with this spirit and don't allow it into your family or your church. It will destroy you. Get rid of it by praying for these people. They need deliverance.

Most churches have encountered attacks from the Jezebel spirit. Those who have discerned and gotten rid of it probably still are enjoying a good strong church. Those who allowed it to stay, or could not discern the spirit, probably lost a lot of members, or have split up and are battling to survive. A lot of people have preached and written on the Jezebel spirit, so I'm not going to repeat them. I am going to address a different kind of spirit attacking our churches today. God showed me a spirit that is more devastating than the Jezebel spirit. It is more dangerous, because it is already in control. It does not have to come into control. This spirit is in every church, everywhere in the world. It is a spirit that can attack and control every person in the church. That includes you and me. It is called the King Saul spirit, and every Christian can be attacked by it.

This spirit wants to use and attack every Christian. It wants to destroy the church and the Christians. We'll talk about that in later chapters. The King Saul spirit is so cunning that few people see it coming, and only a few are recognizing it. This King Saul spirit is slowly killing and destroying our churches and our members. At this point of time, I don't believe that there is any church in the world that is not being attacked by this spirit. Hang in there.

The King Saul spirit not only uses and attacks pastors, praise and worship leaders, and Sunday school teachers, but it also attacks the normal Christian, churchgoing member, *you and me.* Why? Well, we can recognize when a leader in a church is at fault, right? But the normal guy in the pew, trying to destroy the church: that's more difficult to discern. That's why this awful spirit is using the normal church member to destroy the church, and unfortunately, themselves as well.

In this book, I want to show you *who this spirit is, what it looks like, and what its main aim is.* When you read this book, I want you to focus more on your own life than your friend next to you. Forget, for the moment, your spouse, your pastor, the praise and worship leader, and Aunt Martha, who comes to church and leaves early on Sundays. Forget about the other person you think may be a strong candidate to be used by the King Saul spirit. Don't try and figure out who has been misused by this King Saul spirit. Don't try and attach it to someone else. I want you to look and see if perhaps *you* are one of those church members, pastors, leaders, or evangelists that are being attacked. Ask yourself if it is possible that it could attach itself to *you*. Are you being used by it, without even knowing or discerning it? Now don't put down the book. Don't get upset with me. You might be thinking, *"I don't have a King Saul spirit attached to me. I don't have a spirit attached to me at all."* Why don't we check ourselves, check our own lives, and see who or what is attacking us? If everybody does that, then we don't need to worry about the other person, because everyone's looking at their own spiritual lives. Let's check ourselves, to see where we're wrong and where we can do better. Remember the Bible says we must judge ourselves.

> For if we searchingly examined (judged) ourselves [detecting our shortcomings and recognizing our own condition], we should not be judged and penalty decreed [by the divine judgment].
> — 1 Corinthians 11:31 AMP

> For if we would judge ourselves, we would not be judged.
> — 1 Corinthians 11:31

So, let's look at *ourselves* when we're reading this book and judge ourselves according to what God's Word says. Wouldn't you like to be free from certain things that you know are a hindrance to your spiritual life? Of course you would. Even I had to check myself and my ministry to see if the King Saul spirit was attacking us. I did not look at my wife or my daughter; they had to look at their own lives and judge themselves. If you get hold of this principle, it will change your life.

Make sure that this King Saul spirit is not attached to you. If it is, I will show you how to discern it, get rid of it, and stay away from it.

You might be asking the question, *"Why are you calling it the King Saul spirit?"* Well, because this spirit attacked and used King Saul. It destroyed him and made his life a tormenting hell and eventually killed him. It is named after its victim, King Saul.

Summary of this chapter: What is the King Saul spirit? It's not the Jezebel spirit; it's more than that. It has the characteristics of a killing spirit. It attaches itself to all kinds of people, the normal churchgoing member as well as leadership. It could do the same to you and me, if we are not informed of how this spirit works.

Let's see where this monster comes from.

CHAPTER 2

Where Does the King Saul Spirit Come From?

—ɯ—

Now let me warn you: in the beginning, the King Saul spirit looks harmless. This is because it's very deceiving. It does not want anyone to discern it. Its aim is to destroy without being detected. It's a *spirit of death*. Where did it all start? We have to go back in time to find out what happened. In **1 Samuel 8:1-9**, Samuel was getting old, and his sons were not serving God like they should. There was concern over what would happen when Samuel died and his rule fell to them. So the elders came to Samuel and told him that they wanted him to appoint someone to rule over them. Well, since Samuel's sons were not capable of ruling, the people asked Samuel to appoint a king to judge them, just like all the other nations. This displeased Samuel, so he prayed to God and asked Him what to do. Now let's stop right there. It was not a sin to ask for a king. The people were not sinning by asking Samuel to appoint a king to rule over them.

> When you come to the land which the Lord your God is giving you, and possess it and dwell in it, and say, "I will set a king over me like all the nations that are around me," <u>you shall surely set a king over you whom the Lord your God chooses</u>; one from among your brethren you shall set as king over you; you may not set a foreigner over you, who is not your brother. But he shall not multiply horses for himself, nor cause the people to return to Egypt to multiply horses, for the Lord has said to you, "You shall not return that way again."
> Neither shall he multiply wives for himself, lest his heart turn away; nor shall he greatly multiply silver and gold for himself.
> "Also it shall be, when he sits on the throne of his kingdom, that he shall write for himself a copy of this law in a book, from the one before the priests, the Levites. And it shall be with him, and he shall read it all the days of his life, that he may learn to fear the Lord his God and be careful to observe all the words of this law and these statutes, that his heart may not be lifted above his brethren, that he may not turn aside from the commandment to the right hand or to the left, and that he may prolong his days in his kingdom, he and his children in the midst of Israel.
> —Deuteronomy 17:14-20, (emphasis mine)

So asking for a king was not wrong; God had promised them a king. The problem was it was the wrong timing. They were sinning by demanding a king on their own time, which was not God's time. Any time we go ahead of God, my friend, I can guarantee you we're going to mess up. That's what happened to the Israelites.

God then told Samuel to heed the voice of the people, because they were not rejecting him, but rejecting God, who was supposed to reign over them **(1 Sam. 8:7)**. Then God told Samuel to forewarn the people about this king, who they wanted. God warned that the new king was going to cause trouble for them and their families. Samuel did just that and told them that the day would come when they'd cry out to God to help them, but that God would not listen.

The people responded by saying,

> Nevertheless the people refused to obey the voice of Samuel; and they said, "No, but we will have a king over us, that we also may be like all the nations, and that our king may judge us and go out before us and fight our battles" And Samuel heard all the words of the people, and he repeated them in the hearing of the Lord. So the Lord said to Samuel, "Heed their voice, and make them a king." And Samuel said to the men of Israel, "Every man go to his city."
>
> — 1 Samuel 8:19-22

Even after the warning, the people still insisted on having a king rule over them instead of God. In our churches today, a lot of people do the same thing. They want some other kind of spirit to rule instead of the Holy Spirit.

The Israelites had God as a King to rule over them, but their ignorance to ask for an earthly king cost them dearly. Now remember, ignorance is not an excuse. That's why the Word says:

> My people are destroyed for lack of knowledge. Because you have rejected knowledge, I also will reject you from being priest for Me; because you have forgotten the law of your God, I also will forget your children.
>
> —Hosea 4:6

By allowing Saul to become their king, the Israelites did not realize that they were inviting the King Saul spirit into their midst. King Saul, as we will see, originally was a good man and a good king. It wasn't too long after becoming king, though, that his life started changing. He started allowing a spirit to attack him and use him, which ended up destroying him. That's where the *"King Saul spirit"* comes from. It's named after King Saul. In chapter three we will discuss this in detail.

Today, believers are making the same mistake. They're allowing this same spirit into the church, not even knowing that it's there to destroy and kill them. When I say destroy and kill, I'm talking about spiritual, emotional, physical, and mental destruction.

This King Saul spirit is here to destroy your finances, family, job, marriage, church, friends, everything in its path. It doesn't care. Why? Well, it's direct from Satan himself. Remember what Jesus said:

> The thief does not come except to steal, and to <u>kill, and to destroy</u>. I have come that they may have life, and that they may have it more abundantly.
>
> —John 10:10, (emphasis mine)

Everything that kills and destroys is from Satan; that's his character. Everything that's full of life, blessing, victory, breakthrough, healing, and prosperity in abundance is from God.

Summary of this chapter: Where does the King Saul spirit come from? It is a demonic spirit from Satan himself. Remember, this spirit works through the normal churchgoing person and through the leaders. It can work through you and me. Unfortunately, we open the door to this spirit, and then it controls our lives and our churches. Through a lack of knowledge, we allow the King Saul spirit to destroy our churches and the lives of many other precious believers.

It's time to see how this King Saul spirit functions. Let's find out how it can attack and control us.

Where did it all start?

CHAPTER 3

Saul Appointed as King

—·ᴡᴡ·—

Who was Saul? We have to look at this man, chosen by God to be the new king over Israel. Remember, the people asked Samuel to give them a king to rule over them. In **1 Samuel 9:15-17**, God told Samuel to go ahead and appoint a king. Samuel also was informed that God would send him a man from the land of Benjamin. When Samuel saw Saul, God told him it was the right man, the one that God had **chosen.** He was the man that was to save the Israelites from the Philistines, their enemies. Let's look at this carefully.

We learn more about Saul in **1 Samuel 9:1-10**. He was a Benjamite, the son of Kish, a mighty man of power (meaning wealth). Saul came from a family that was rich and had power, influence, and a strong army. Saul himself was a tall, handsome young man, physically strong. He was taller and better looking than any other person. Saul came from a good strong solid family, with a strong powerful father.

The Word tells us that Saul's father had donkeys that were lost. Saul was sent to find them. On his way, he had trouble finding the donkeys and wanted to return home. Saul's servant suggested that they go to the seer (a prophet of God) to find out if he could help them find the donkeys before they gave up. This is how Saul met Samuel the prophet. This also is when God showed Samuel that Saul was the man to be anointed king over Israel. Samuel told Saul that the donkeys would be found and not to be anxious. He then invited Saul to come and eat with him. Afterward, Samuel anointed Saul as king over Israel.

I want you to get this. Saul was a normal, good man, a strong man, doing good for himself. He was a likeable guy. If he had walked into a church, people would like him. Just a normal guy, as we see in our churches today.

Let's look at some facts about Saul. Then, let's compare those facts to *you and me,* average church members. We have to follow the story of King Saul so that we can see how this spirit attacked and used him. This is very important, because it will also show us who the King Saul spirit can attack and control.

Facts about Saul:

1) Saul was **chosen** by God, to be the next king over Israel. **1 Samuel 10:24:** *"And Samuel said to all the people, 'Do you see him whom **the Lord has chosen,** that there is no one like him among all*

the people?' So all the people shouted and said, 'Long live the king!'" (emphasis mine).

2) Saul **was anointed** by God, to rule over His people. **1 Samuel 10:1:** *"Then Samuel took a flask of oil and poured it on his head, and kissed him and said: 'Is it not because **the Lord has anointed you** commander over His inheritance?'"* (emphasis mine).

3) The Spirit of the Lord **came upon** Saul. **1 Samuel 10:6:** *"Then **the Spirit of the Lord will come upon you** and you will prophesy with them and be turned into another man"* (emphasis mine).

4) Saul started to **prophesy. 1 Samuel 10:6:** *"Then the Spirit of the Lord will come upon you, **and you will prophesy** with them and be turned into another man"* (emphasis mine).

5) Saul was turned into **another man** (he was changed into a new man). **1 Samuel 10:6:** *"Then the Spirit of the Lord will come upon you, and you will prophesy with them **and be turned into another man"** (emphasis mine).

6) God **was with** Saul. **1 Samuel 10:7:** *"And let it be, when these signs come to you, that you do as the occasion demands; **for God is with you"*** (emphasis mine).

7) Saul received a **new heart. 1 Samuel 10:9:** *"So it was, when he had turned his back to go from Samuel that **God gave him another heart**; and all those signs came to pass that day"* (emphasis mine).

My friend, this man, who had these characteristics, was attacked and used by the King Saul spirit. This demonic spirit attached itself to King Saul, and he allowed it to control him, without even realizing it. Now, this King Saul spirit is everywhere, and it's attacking and controlling the children of God, too. It started with King Saul and is still around today, doing exactly what it started thousands of years ago.

I don't know about you, but these facts about King Saul fascinate me. I thought he was a bad guy. Man, he did terrible things, according to me. All I could remember was that he wanted to kill David. When I began to study further, I found out that in the beginning Saul was a good, normal person, just like most of the Christians I know. Yes, he did bad things, but not from the beginning. Before being crowned king, he was a good guy from a good family background, living a good solid life, with a good job, doing well for himself. Then God decided that Saul would be the one to save the Israelites from their enemies, the Philistines. God chose Saul and anointed him as king. The Spirit of the Lord came upon him. He began to prophesy. Saul was turned into another man. God was with him. Guess what, God even gave Saul another heart, a new heart. The man changed from being the old Saul to a brand new man with new characteristics, known as King Saul.

Now don't get me wrong here, but this sounds too familiar to me. We know that in the Old Testament, people did not get born again, right? Nevertheless, if you look at what happened to Saul, it sounds just like the modern-day, born-again Christian. If Saul was living in the year 2009, having these qualities or facts we've just mentioned, we would most probably say he was a born-again Christian.

Let's look at the facts of a born-again Christian today and compare current believers to King Saul: they are almost identical. You see, this is the kind of person that the King Saul spirit attacks and uses: people that seem like good, born-again believers. It not only attacks people who seem to have problems already. No, I'm talking about people like you and me, born-again Christians, the ones from whom you would never expect it. These are the people that this King Saul spirit will use and attach itself to. We are the people that have to watch out for this King Saul spirit. It's so deceiving; we would never expect it to attack our neighbor, or attack us. If it could attack Saul—a chosen, anointed man of God, who had the Holy Spirit on him and could prophesy, having God with him, being changed into another man, a different man with a new heart—I'm telling you, it can attack you and me as well. Saul did not even realize that by becoming king, he had stepped into a spiritual battle that would change his whole life forever. The moment he was made king, the King Saul spirit started to attach itself to him. What happened to Israel and

King Saul is history, and we'll take a closer look at it later on.

Now let's take a look at the facts of a Christian. You'll see that they are almost the same as the facts of King Saul.

Facts about born-again Christians:

1) God has **chosen us,** too, to be His people, born again. **1 Peter 2:9-10:** *"But you are a __chosen generation__, a royal priesthood, a holy nation, His own __special people__, that you may proclaim the praises of Him who called you out of darkness into His marvelous light; who once were not a people but are now the people of God, who had not obtained mercy but now have obtained mercy"* (emphasis mine). Can you see that God has chosen you and me to be His special people? God wants us, just like Saul, to save His lost people. He wants them saved, healed, and delivered from the enemy, Satan. He wants to use us. He's chosen us, just like He chose Saul. God has chosen some of us to be pastors, evangelists, teachers, and prophets. Some of us are Sunday school teachers, some are youth leaders, and some are praise and worship leaders. Some of us are just chosen to help around the church, cut the grass and clean up. Some do the cooking for special events. Some of us are chosen to be prayer warriors and intercessors. All of us are chosen to be born-again, so that we can join the saints in heaven one day. All

of us are chosen to be witnesses for Jesus. Like Saul, we are chosen for a specific task.

2) God has **anointed us** as well, just like He **anointed** King Saul. Do you realize you are **the anointed of God? You have an anointing** from God. **1 John 2:20:** *"But you have an anointing from the Holy One, and you know all things."* **1 John 2:27:** *"But the anointing which you have received from Him abides in you, and you do not need that anyone teach you; but as the same anointing teaches you concerning all things, and is true, and is not a lie, and just as it has taught you, you will abide in Him."* God anointed Saul so that he could save the Israelites from the Philistines. God has anointed you and me to be witnesses, so that people can be saved from the devil and his demons, and from going to hell. Every one of us is an anointed child of God. As Saul was *anointed by God*, so are we *anointed by God*.

3) The **Spirit of the Lord is upon us.** In the Old Testament days, the Spirit of God came upon the people. Today the Holy Spirit is living in us. **Luke 4:18-19:** *"The <u>**Spirit of the Lord is upon Me**</u>, Because He has <u>**anointed**</u> Me to preach the gospel to the poor; He has sent Me to heal the broken-hearted, to proclaim liberty to the captives and recovery of sight to the blind, to set at liberty those who are oppressed; to proclaim the acceptable year of the Lord"* (emphasis mine). Jesus quoted this scripture and so can we. We have the

Holy Spirit of God. When we get born-again, the Holy Spirit comes and joins itself to our spirit. **1 Corinthians 6:17:** *"But he who is joined to the Lord is one spirit with Him."* **Acts 1:8:** *"But you shall receive power when the **Holy Spirit has come upon you;** and you shall be witnesses to Me in Jerusalem, and in all Judea and Samaria, and to the end of the earth"* (emphasis mine). We have the Holy Spirit in us, just like Saul had the Holy Spirit in him.

Saul is very similar to us; we all have been chosen by God. We're all anointed by God and have the Holy Spirit. Very interesting!

4) **The believer also can prophesy.** As believers, we have the Holy Spirit, who can give us the *gift of prophecy.* Most of us can prophesy any time we want to, just by prophesying the Word of God over people, by speaking the Word of truth into their lives. Just like Saul started to prophesy, so can we as believers. **Romans 12:6:** *"Having then gifts differing according to the grace that is given to us, let us use them: if prophecy, **let us prophesy** in proportion to our faith"* (emphasis mine). **2 Peter 1:19-21:** *"And so we have the **prophetic word** confirmed, which you do well to heed as a light that shines in a dark place, until the day dawns and the morning star rises in your hearts; knowing this first, that **no prophecy of Scripture** is of any private interpretation, **for prophecy** never came by the will of man, but holy men of*

God spoke as they were moved by the Holy Spirit"
(emphasis mine).

5) When we become born-again, we are **turned into another man**. Saul was turned into **another man,** too. Paul wrote in **2 Corinthians 5:17:** *"Therefore, if anyone is in Christ, he is a <u>**new creation;**</u> old things have passed away; behold, <u>**all things have become new"**</u>* (emphasis mine). Paul basically said that we became another person: a new creature in and through Christ Jesus, who saved us through His precious blood. At this point, both Saul and you and I are chosen by God, anointed by God. We have the Holy Spirit in us and on us, we can prophesy, we're tuned into another new man, or person. We and Saul: we're pretty much in the same boat, aren't we?

6) **God is with us,** just as He was with Saul. Why? So that we can do that what He has called us to do. We have to work for Him and save His people from going to hell.

   Joshua 1:9: *"Have I not commanded you? Be strong and of good courage; do not be afraid, nor be dismayed, for the <u>**Lord your God is with you wherever you go**</u>.*" (emphasis mine).

   You see, God is always with us, just as He was with Saul. In everything we do, we can always be assured, knowing that God is with us.

7) As born-again Christians, we have received a **new heart**. The old heart has been taken out

and replaced with a brand new heart from God. Again we quote **2 Corinthians 5:17:** *"Therefore, if anyone is in Christ, he is <u>a **new creation**</u>; old things have passed away; behold, <u>**all things have become new"**</u>* (emphasis mine). If all things became new, then so have our hearts become new. God has given us a brand new heart.

This is how I got saved: God chose me, He anointed me, and I received the Holy Spirit. I prophesied the Word; I was turned into another man, who had God with me all the time. I had received a new heart. Now I was ready to be used in God's plan for my life.

God has positioned you, too, my friend, so that you can also be used in His plan to save the world and set it free from the bondages of Satan. The question is: are we doing this, are we getting people saved, or are you and I being attacked and used by the King Saul spirit, just like King Saul was attacked and used by it? Let's find out.

The King Saul spirit attached itself to King Saul, a chosen and anointed man of God, full of the Holy Spirit. God was with him, turned him into another man, allowed him to prophesy, and gave him a new heart. If that could happen to King Saul, then I'm sure that it can happen to *you and me* as well, the born-again children of God. Why not? We both have the same characteristics, right? I hope you understand this. That's why it's so important not to look at other people, but to identify this spirit in our own lives first.

Summary of this chapter: We are basically in the same boat with King Saul. Both of us have the same characteristics at this point of time. Let's summarize the similarities between King Saul and the believer.

Facts:

King Saul

1) Chosen—(1 Sam. 10:24)
2) Anointed—(1 Sam. 10:1)
3) Indwelled by the Holy Spirit—(1 Sam. 10:6)
4) Accompanied by God—(1 Sam. 10:7)
5) Prophesying—(1 Sam. 10:6)
6) Turned into another man—(1 Sam. 10:6)
7) Given a new heart—(1 Sam. 10:9)

Born-Again Believers (you and I)

1) Chosen—(1 Pet. 2:9)
2) Anointed—(1 John 2:20, 27)
3) Indwelled by the Holy Spirit—(Luke 4:18)
4) Accompanied by God—(Heb. 13:5)
5) Prophesying—(Rom. 12:6)
6) Turned into another man and
7) Given a new heart —(2 Cor. 5:17)

We are not immune to this King Saul spirit. At this point, most of you are asking, *"Well, what does this King Saul spirit do? How did it attack King Saul?"*

Let's go see how it developed and when it started showing up, through an anointed, chosen man of God, the king of Israel, *King Saul.*

CHAPTER 4

Before the Change

—∿∿—

I want you to know that before the King Saul spirit started manifesting in his life, there were some good qualities in King Saul. Let's take a look at them. Now don't forget that King Saul was chosen and anointed. He received the Holy Spirit. God was with him. He was turned into another man. He prophesied and received a new heart. According to these characteristics, we can assume that everything King Saul did in the first two years of his reign as king was good and inspired by the Holy Spirit. Let's look at some of King Saul's characteristics early in his reign.

1) <u>Saul was humble.</u> He had a humble spirit. Remember, Samuel invited Saul to have lunch with him, to tell him that God had chosen him to be king. Well, Saul replied humbly:

And Saul answered and said, "Am I not a Benjamite, of the smallest of the tribes of

Israel, and my family the least of all the families of the tribe of Benjamin? Why then do you speak like this to me?"

—1 Samuel 9:21

When they called all the tribes together to appoint the new king, Saul was nowhere to be found. He's like the guy you ask to do a special song Sunday morning, while the offering is taken up; but he never shows up, because he feels intimidated by the song leader, who can sing much better than he can. It's like the lady you ask to teach a Sunday school class. She's so humble; she thinks someone else should do the job, because she's not qualified enough. Look what happened when they called Saul to announce him as the new king.

When he had caused the tribe of Benjamin to come near by their families, the family of Matri was chosen. And Saul the son of Kish was chosen. But when they sought him, he could not be found. Therefore they inquired of the Lord further, "Has the man come here yet?" And the Lord answered, "There he is, hidden among the equipment." So they ran and brought him from there; and when he stood among the people, he was taller than any of the people from his shoulders upward. And Samuel said to all the people, "Do you see him whom the Lord has chosen, that there is no one like him among all the people?" So

42

all the people shouted and said, "Long live the king!"

—1 Samuel 10:21-24

You see, the man was so humble that he hid from the people and from Samuel. He thought that he was *not good enough* to be chosen. Many Christians are the same way, and most of us have this quality in the beginning of our Christian lives. We are humble toward people and situations. *"Oh Lord, no, not me. Use someone else, God"* Maybe you've been there before.

2) <u>Saul was a man of peace.</u> When some of the people, or rebels, despised King Saul, he just kept quiet and let them go. He kept the peace. He could have made things difficult for them, but he had a spirit of peace. He did not want to harm his own people. The same with us; most of us don't want to harm our brothers and sisters in our churches, right? We want peace.

But some rebels said, "How can this man save us?" So they despised him, and brought him no presents. But he held his peace.

—1 Samuel 10:27

3) <u>Saul was a helping man.</u> The people of Jabesh Gilead were troubled, because the man who was about to make a covenant with them, Nahash the Ammonite, wanted to take out all

the people's right eyes. This deed would have been a reproach to Israel. What a cruel plan! When King Saul heard this, he was angry, and the Holy Spirit came upon him. King Saul then got his people together, and they went out to help Jabesh. King Saul and his army killed the Ammonites, who were going to harm Jabesh. We, too, as Christians should help each other. Most believers want to help, and should be helpful where they can.

Then the Spirit of God came upon Saul when he heard this news, and his anger was greatly aroused.

—1 Samuel 11:6

And they said to the messengers who came, "Thus you shall say to the men of Jabesh Gilead: 'Tomorrow, by the time the sun is hot, you shall have help.'" Then the messengers came and reported it to the men of Jabesh, and they were glad.

—1 Samuel 11:9

4) <u>Saul was not a man of revenge.</u> After this victory over the Ammonites, some of the people suggested they get the rebels together and kill them, because the rebels did not believe that King Saul could lead them to victory. King Saul wanted nothing to do with such behavior, and gave God the glory for the

victory. No revenge. Remember, revenge has no place in the life of a believer.

Then the people said to Samuel, "Who is he who said, 'Shall Saul reign over us?' Bring the men, that we may put them to death." But Saul said, "Not a man shall be put to death this day, for today the Lord has accomplished salvation in Israel."

—1 Samuel 11:12-13

King Saul was a good man at this point of time. He was doing and saying the right things. If only he and the people could have stayed that way. Everything would have been great. Even Samuel told them that they could prosper and have good days ahead of them, together with King Saul, their king. He told them how to do it as well.

If you fear the Lord and serve Him and obey His voice, and do not rebel against the commandment of the Lord, then both you and the king who reigns over you will continue following the Lord your God.

However, if you do not obey the voice of the Lord, but rebel against the commandment of the Lord, then the hand of the Lord will be against you, as it was against your fathers.

—1 Samuel 12:14-15, (emphasis mine)

I believe with all my heart that King Saul could have taken Israel to great victories through the power of the Holy Spirit, if he had done what God called him to do. Israel and their king could have prospered and had a good life. They could have had God on their side in every situation. The problem was the King Saul spirit showed up and messed up every-thing. It attacked and started using King Saul.

The positive qualities mentioned above changed when King Saul gave in to the King Saul spirit. Many of us have the same good qualities as King Saul, but they also can change if we, too, give in to the attacks of this spirit.

Let's see how the change took place, and when it started.

CHAPTER 5

The Change in King Saul

FEAR

—⁓—

What was the change that took place in King Saul's life? What did he do wrong to let this demon spirit attack and destroy him? He made a lot of mistakes, and we're going to look at how it started and developed. Eventually you'll see how this King Saul spirit destroyed King Saul. At the same time, we'll see how we can get into the same trouble King Saul did if we make the same mistakes. Let's look at the first characteristic of the King Saul spirit.

In **1 Samuel 13:1-7,** we see that King Saul had been reigning for two years when he decided to attack the Philistines. Now, I really believe that in those two years he was reigning with the wisdom and help of the Holy Spirit. Everything was going according to plan.

Jonathan, his son, then attacked a garrison of the Philistines. This made them so mad that the Philistine army gathered together their soldiers, multitudes of them, and they came together to attack Israel. This made the men of Israel afraid. They were distressed, seeing all the Philistines coming against them. So they decided to flee in different directions. The Israelite army was scattered everywhere. This left King Saul and six hundred of his men behind in Gilgal.

> Then the Philistines gathered together to fight with Israel, thirty thousand chariots and six thousand horsemen, and people as the sand which is on the seashore in multitude. And they came up and encamped in Michmash, to the east of Beth Aven. When the men of Israel saw that they were in danger (for the people were distressed), then the people hid in caves, in thickets, in rocks, in holes, and in pits.
> —1 Samuel 13:5-6

> Then Samuel arose and went up from Gilgal to Gibeah of Benjamin. And Saul numbered the people present with him, about six hundred men.
> —1 Samuel 13:15

Now remember that Samuel had told King Saul to go to Gilgal and wait there seven days, until he, Samuel would come and tell him what to do.

> You shall go down before me to Gilgal; and surely I will come down to you to offer burnt offerings and make sacrifices of peace offer-

ings. Seven days you shall wait, till I come to you and show you what you should do.
—1 Samuel 10:8

So here was King Saul, at Gilgal, waiting for Samuel to come to him. He had six hundred men left, while the rest of the soldiers were hiding away from the enemy in fear.

The problem was that the Philistines were ready to attack and kill, and Samuel was not showing up. This put fear in the people, and they scattered. So instead of depending on God and His promises, as he did in the first two years of his reign, King Saul gave in to the King Saul spirit. How did he do it, and what did he do wrong? What was the first sign of the King Saul spirit? What was the change like? I need you to get this, because this is the first characteristic of the King Saul spirit. King Saul and the people became **afraid.** Allowing **fear** in their lives was their first mistake. This fear opened the door to the King Saul spirit. They became fearful when they saw the multitude of Philistines. King Saul and the soldiers basically gave in to the spirit of fear.

That's when I realized that the King Saul spirit starts most of its attacks with fear.

If it can get people to fear, then the destruction can start. Fear, my friend, is one of the King Saul spirit's first attempts to destroy the believers and the church. Why? Well, fear ends in destruction, if we don't control it. Fear is a killer, my friend.

The moment a Christian starts fearing, the King Saul spirit shows up. Have you ever been afraid?

Well, of course you have. So has everyone else. Everyone has had some kind of fear in their life. But God said we must not fear. Why?

> For God has not given us a spirit of fear, but of power and of love and of a sound mind.
> —2 Timothy 1:7

Over and over in the Word of God, we are told: *"be not afraid"; "do not fear"; "have no fear";* and *"fear not."* God does not want us to fear the situations we are going through, but to rather have faith in Him. We should put our faith, or *confidence, reliance, assurance, our trust,* in God. He's the One who's on our side, so we don't have to worry or fear. We have the Holy Spirit power in us, we have God's love abiding in us, and we have a sound mind, or the mind of Christ. That's power, so why fear? The bottom line is that God says the battle is His and not ours; He wants to fight on our behalf. What a blessing to know that!

Now remember that just as the King Saul spirit attacked King Saul because of fear, it can attack you and me as well when we have fear in our lives. Remember that humble young man who was asked to sing a special song on Sunday morning? He never sang, you know. Fear stepped in, and he asked the pastor to release him. The lady that was asked to teach the Sunday school class never made it. She was so afraid of what people would say that she actually got sick. The pastor had to find someone else. Where does this leave you and me? Well, we have to stop fearing; it opens the door to the King Saul spirit.

King Saul had to fight the Philistines; no wonder he was afraid. Nevertheless, he didn't have to be afraid. God was going to show him, through Samuel the prophet, what to do at Gilgal. God was going to fight for them. Saul didn't have to be fearful and take matters into his own hands.

Summary of this chapter: Well, the change came. The attack of the King Saul spirit started. A small little mistake, being afraid, changed King Saul's whole life. This was the first mistake the king made; he allowed *fear* to come into his life. This was the beginning of the destruction of King Saul. The King Saul spirit saw the opening, and it used the opportunity to attach itself to King Saul. It put fear in the heart of the king. Let's see how this led to the next characteristic of the King Saul spirit.

CHAPTER 6

The Change in King Saul

IMPATIENCE

—⟋⟍—

King Saul had allowed fear to come into his life. The King Saul spirit had attacked him, and his downfall had just begun. You see, the King Saul spirit is very cunning. The moment it put fear in King Saul's life, it made way for the second characteristic to come into place. The King Saul spirit let King Saul become *impatient.*

When people become fearful, they start to panic or worry. Some stress out. Others throw tantrums. Most of us just get impatient. Fear usually leads to impatience. Yes, my friend, this might be a shocker to some. When fear enters in, and you don't keep it together or let God handle the situation, impatience will follow, I promise. When you're impatient, you aren't thinking clearly. I know; I've been there. If you are honest, you will agree, right?

What happened? Well, anytime that people become impatient, they do the things they should not do, and they get into trouble. Come on, so many of us have done that. We get impatient with things, or situations, or people, or even with God. We take matters into our own hands, and then we mess up. That's what King Saul did. Now this King Saul spirit waited two years before it attached itself to King Saul. So don't be deceived; it will wait for an opportune time to attack and attach itself to you and me as well. This man was chosen, anointed of God, had the Spirit of God, was accompanied by God, had been turned into another man, and was prophesying with a new heart. Then he made a little mistake. He feared and then became *impatient*. Was that such a big sin? If you look at it that way, we all could say we see impatience in our lives. That's normal. Well, you're right, and that's my point. This King Saul spirit already has attacked most of us: the normal, churchgoing, born-again Christians. Let me tell you something: every Christian in this whole wide world has been attacked by this King Saul spirit. I don't think there is anybody who can say they've never been afraid or impatient. No one, however, has ever been told that it's part of the King Saul spirit's strategy to destroy them.

The impatience that King Saul demonstrated seemed normal, but the truth is that it's not part of the fruit of the Spirit. Patience is. So being impatient is not normal; it's carnal. If we are walking in the Spirit, we should be patient. Although it might seem insignificant, this little bit of impatience was part of King Saul's downfall. It was part of the King Saul spirit's attack on God's chosen, anointed man. Why does this spirit choose impatience to destroy our lives? Well, impatience is destructive, just like fear. If the enemy can get you to fear, he knows you're going to get impatient. Together, they make a powerful destructive force. This spirit knows he's got us in the corner. Every time we get impatient, we open the door to get into trouble.

Let me help you. Have you ever driven down the road in a bit of a hurry, going a little over the speed limit? Then, all of the sudden, in front of you is a car . . . an old car. It's a bit rusted, with one of the wheels buckling. Inside is an old lady. Guess what — she's doing the speed limit. Now you don't like that, because you're in a hurry. The problem is you're not allowed to pass her, because there's a solid line running down the middle of the road. As a matter of fact, there's a sign that says, "No passing." So you're born again, right? You want to do the right thing; you're just waiting for the right time to pass her. The problem is that there is not going to be a right time. For the next five miles, the road has a "no passing" sign posted. So you start to worry. You're going to be late for your appointment. Fear rises up in you. This is the first mistake, and an attack coming your way. So you start speaking to the old lady. She can't hear you, but you speak to her in any case. You're busy telling her that you're going to be late and she'd better move over. You're going to lose the business deal if you can't pass her; fear is increasing. The shoulder is wide enough for her to pull over so you can pass her. Why doesn't she move? Does she realize you're going to miss your appointment? Does she know what she's doing? *"This can't be happening,"* you think.

"Come on, you old people should not even be on the road," you say. *"Where did you get your license, woman, at Walmart?"* Man, you're really giving it to her. So you get a bit impatient. You start speaking with your hands as well, not only with your mouth. Signs are being given to the old lady. Now, remember, she's not in the wrong. She's doing her fifty-five miles per hour, which is the speed limit. So after a few miles, you're really impatient. Now you're really hot, mad. You decide you're going to do something about this situation. You can hardly see ahead of you, but who cares. You do it. You step on the gas and pass her, while you're still giving her the lip and the hand signs. You've passed her successfully, and you're happy with your assignment. Now you have to get a move on, because you're late. So you're stepping on the gas, smiling all the way.

"I've done it! The stupid old lady, what's wrong with her?" you say to yourself. Well, all of a sudden you hear a funny sound. Behind you is a car with disco lights on the roof, flashing blue. Someone's following you. But you know that sound, and it's not a mobile disco, so you pull over. *"What did I do wrong, officer?"* you ask in your most friendly tone. Come on, you know what you did. You passed the old lady on a non-passing road, and you were speeding. You've messed up, and now you're fined a lot of money. Why? The reason is because you feared, then got impatient, and took things into your

own hands. You got into trouble. Be glad you didn't have a wreck and kill yourself and the old lady, too. You could have died and killed other people. That's what this King Saul spirit wants in the long run.

How many times have you and I been impatient and gotten into trouble? The question is: are we going to allow this King Saul spirit to take over our lives and destroy us, or are we going to recognize it, bind it, and loose it from our lives? The choice is ours. We know when we're fearful, and we know when we're impatient. It doesn't have to destroy us or our churches. We have the power to resist this spirit in Jesus' name, don't we?

Now, King Saul allowed this King Saul spirit to take over his life. After he became **afraid,** he became **impatient**. What did he do wrong? He became impatient and **self-willed**. He stepped into the office of the prophet Samuel by offering burnt offerings to God. That was not his duty, but the prophet's. Why did he do it? He was afraid of the Philistines. The fact that Samuel wasn't showing up didn't help either. He felt compelled to take action. The result: **pride** stepped in. This made him act foolishly in God's eyes, and he became **disobedient** toward God. Oh my, what a sequence this King Saul spirit follows: fear, impatience, self-will, pride, disobedience, and foolishness. Let's look at the Scriptures.

> Then he waited seven days, according to the time set by Samuel. But Samuel did not come to Gilgal; and the people were scattered from him. So Saul said, "Bring a burnt offering and

peace offerings here to me." And he offered the burnt offering. Now it happened, as soon as he had finished presenting the burnt offering, that Samuel came; and Saul went out to meet him, that he might greet him. And Samuel said, "What have you done?" And Saul said, "When I saw that the people were scattered from me, and that you did not come within the days appointed, and that the Philistines gathered together at Michmash, then I said, 'The Philistines will now come down on me at Gilgal, and I have not made supplication to the Lord.' Therefore I felt compelled, and offered a burnt offering." And Samuel said to Saul, "<u>You have done foolishly</u>. You have <u>not kept the commandment</u> of the Lord your God, which He commanded you. For now the Lord would have established your kingdom over Israel forever. But now your kingdom shall not continue. The Lord has sought for Himself a man after His own heart, and the Lord has commanded him to be commander over His people, because you have not kept what the Lord commanded you."

—1 Samuel 13:8-14, (emphasis mine)

This King Saul spirit made King Saul *impatient,* which led to being *self-willed,* all because he was *afraid of* the enemy.

In what ways was he self-willed, prideful, and foolish? Why was he disobedient? Well, he offered up the burnt offering, instead of waiting for Samuel to do it. His impatience led to his disobedience. I can just hear him saying, *"Well, if Samuel doesn't want to come, then I'll do the job. I'm not going to wait for some prophet that promised he would come, and now he's late, or not even coming. I mean, I'm the king now; I can do whatever I want to do. It's been seven days now, so where is Samuel?"* Pride, oh pride, what a great fall awaited King Saul! This whole deal, Samuel said later, was disobedience to God. Saul had not done what God had commanded of him. King Saul had acted foolishly, taking matters into his own hands.

Keep in mind that Samuel had warned the people and King Saul that if they feared God (respecting God, have reverence toward God, being obedient to God, giving God honor), then they would have God's blessing and protection and support. Obviously, it lasted only for two years, and then the King Saul spirit showed up.

> If you fear the Lord and serve Him and obey His voice, and do not rebel against the commandment of the Lord, then both you and the king who reigns over you will continue following the Lord your God. However, if you do not obey the voice of the Lord, but rebel against the commandment of the Lord, then the hand of the Lord will be against you, as it was against your fathers.
> —1 Samuel 12:14-15, (emphasis mine)

How does it affect us? Well, as born-again believers of God, the King Saul spirit does exactly the same thing to us. It wants the child of God to get impatient. Why? So that you and I will be unable to wait for God to act, but instead take matters into our own hands.

I'm going to say it again. If only we can take control of this impatient spirit attacking us. If only we can realize it's not from God, but from the devil. If we can stop being impatient, I believe a lot of our problems can be solved. Unfortunately, we allow fear to step in and torment us. We get impatient, self-willed, and prideful, because we think we can do it ourselves. We act foolishly, become disobedient to God or authorities, and we're in deep trouble.

So, do you think this King Saul spirit is attacking our churches and Christians? We are definitely choice candidates, you know. There are born-again Christians today that want to achieve great things in their lives. They want to be pastors, leaders, teachers, or evangelists. They want to sing in the praise team or lead the worship. They want to be on the deacon board. Some want to be Sunday school teachers. Now there is really nothing wrong in having aspirations in life or achieving certain goals. The problem is . . . when people don't get what they want, fear can enter in. They think the enemy's going to steal their dream. They become impatient with the people who have to help them, because they think it's taking too long. All of a sudden, it looks like they might not achieve their goals. Some people even become impatient with God. They become self-willed and prideful.

They start acting foolishly, doing things their own way, and trouble is soon to follow. Many people cannot wait for God to show up and help them, so they start doing things according to their own ideas and mess up. They ignore the warnings and instructions in God's Word. They become disobedient and start acting foolishly, just like King Saul did. Does it sound familiar? That's how easy it is for this King Saul spirit to deceive and trap any one of us.

Summary of this chapter: If only we can recognize this King Saul spirit, it would be so easy to get rid of it. Actually we could. We know when we're fearful, impatient, self-willed, and prideful. We know when we're disobedient and when we're acting foolishly, right? That's why I'm telling you about this spirit. Most people have never thought of this. So you might say, "It's not so bad." Hang in there; this is just the beginning. It would be easy to get out at this point of time, if only you and I would realize what's attacking us. Most of us have never had this knowledge, and we've been deceived and attacked and used by this King Saul spirit without even knowing it. Let's look at the next characteristic of the King Saul spirit.

CHAPTER 7

The Change in King Saul

DISTRESSED AND TROUBLED

—◆—

Our story picks up in **1 Samuel 14:1-23**. Remember that the Philistines were going to attack Israel. The people and King Saul became afraid. King Saul had instruction to wait for Samuel, but became impatient. He became self-willed and full of pride. He became disobedient to what God had told him to do and acted foolishly in the eyes of God. While the whole of Israel and their king were waiting for the enemy to attack, Jonathan, King Saul's son, decided to go enemy hunting. Some of you might not have known this, but the soldiers of Israel did not have any spears or swords. No wonder King Saul's army was afraid of the Philistines. Only Jonathan and King Saul had weapons. This shows that God was going to do a supernatural thing in their lives and defeat the Philistines for them.

Now there was no blacksmith to be found throughout all the land of Israel, for the Philistines said, "Lest the Hebrews make swords or spears." But all the Israelites would go down to the Philistines to sharpen each man's plowshare, his mattock, his axe, and his sickle; and the charge for a sharpening was a pim [about two thirds shekel weight] for the plowshares, the mattocks, the forks, and the axes, and to set the points of the goads. So it came about, on the day of battle, that there was <u>neither sword nor spear</u> found in the hand <u>of any of the people</u> who were with Saul and Jonathan. <u>But they were found with Saul and Jonathan his son.</u>

—1 Samuel 13:19-22, (emphasis mine)

Why did they have no weapons? Well, the Israelites had no blacksmiths. The Philistines made sure there were none, so that the Israelites could not fight them. Without weapons, they were defenseless. Until the time of Saul, the Philistines had a monopoly on the melting of iron, and the Israelites had to take their tools to them for sharpening. The Israelites went down to the Philistine camp every year and had to pay to sharpen their <u>plowshares</u> *(the iron tip of the plow, which enters the earth),* their <u>mattocks</u> *(an agricultural implement like a pickax, with a wide point for grubbing up and digging out roots and stones),* and their <u>axes and sickles</u>. They had to do this so they could work in their fields.

Let's get back to **1 Samuel 14:1-23.** Jonathan and his armor-bearer decided to go visit the Philistines. They had weapons, remember. Jonathan wanted to go and kill some of these Philistines, and he did. He and his armor-bearer killed about twenty Philistines that day,

(1 Sam. 14:14). The men, who saw Jonathan and his armor-bearer scrambling up the rock, had been surprised and were killed. The spectacle of twenty corpses would suggest to others that they were attacked by a numerous force. At the same moment Jonathan attacked, God caused an earthquake to take place, which shook the rest of the garrison and the three bands of spoilers that had already left the camp **(1 Sam. 14:15).** Now remember, there were watchmen who monitored the Philistines and reported their movements to King Saul. All of a sudden, confusion broke loose. They saw the Philistines starting to run everywhere, confused, "melting away" **(1 Sam. 14:16).** There was a lot of noise in the enemy camp. They were beating each other up and killing each other. Something had happened.

What a God we serve! Just when you thought that Israel was going to be destroyed, God intervened. Instead of praising God, King Saul requested a roll call. He wanted to know who was absent. To his surprise, Jonathan and his armor-bearer were missing. King Saul then assembled the people, and they all went to battle against the Philistines. But when they got there, they saw that the Philistines were killing each other. That's how God saved the

Israelites that day. However, King Saul was still a self-willed, prideful man.

So at this point, the next characteristic of the King Saul spirit showed up. King Saul had **distressed** and **troubled** the people. How? He had placed the people under an oath. Nobody was allowed to eat until the evening after Saul's vengeance on his enemy. He put a curse on his own people. If people could have eaten freely, they would have been stronger and could have fought better. You see people who fear become impatient, self-willed, prideful, disobedient, and they act foolishly. Then they start distressing and troubling people by cursing and harming them. Many times Christians in churches do the same thing. They curse their brothers and sisters in the Lord through the things they say or do.

> And the men of Israel were <u>distressed</u> that day, for Saul had placed the people under oath, saying, "<u>Cursed</u> is the man who eats any food until evening, before I have taken vengeance on my enemies." So none of the people tasted food.
> — 1 Samuel 14:24, (emphasis mine)

Jonathan did not know about this oath, and he went ahead and ate some honey. It brightened his countenance. When the people saw him eat, they told Jonathan that King Saul had said anyone who ate would be cursed. Jonathan replied that his dad was **troubling** the people. He knew that the people could have fought better if they were allowed to eat of the spoil. When you and I allow this King Saul spirit to attack us, we will be allowing the same thing. We will make those around us distressed and troubled, too. Most people who are attacked by the King Saul spirit want to tell other people what to do and not to do. They trouble people. This spirit is always out there, putting demands on other people, and making trouble for them.

The people got so troubled and distressed from hunger that when they eventually got to the food, they sinned. They ate food with blood, which was a sin in those days.

> And the people rushed on the spoil, and took sheep, oxen, and calves, and slaughtered them on the ground; and the <u>people ate them with the blood.</u> Then they told Saul, saying, "Look, <u>the people are sinning against the Lord</u> by <u>eating with the blood</u>!" So he said, "You have dealt treacherously; roll a large stone to me this day."
>   — 1 Samuel 14:32-33, (emphasis mine)

This King Saul spirit can make you sin, but it also puts other people in the position to sin. After this incident, King Saul was mad at Jonathan because he broke the oath by eating. Here is a bad sign of this King Saul spirit. King Saul had no pity, even on his own son. He was prepared to kill his own son because he broke the oath. You see, anyone who goes against this spirit can be wiped out and killed. The

King Saul spirit wants to kill, remember. That's its aim: to destroy people, even if it's family.

Thank God the people rescued Jonathan by telling Saul that Jonathan had a great victory over those twenty Philistines. He did not deserve to die. If it was not for those people, Jonathan would have been killed that day by his own dad. What a wicked spirit! Now people who are attacked by the King Saul spirit will do the same thing. It might not cause physical death, but will cause so much spiritual harm to people that they will backslide. It doesn't care who you are. Don't be deceived: this is a killing spirit. The people being used by this King Saul spirit won't even feel bad if they destroy a church or another Christian.

We must remember that this King Saul spirit is out there to destroy God's children and His church. This spirit is out to destroy you and me. The King Saul spirit wants to attach itself to us, so that we can hurt other people, too. It wants to use us to destroy God's church and His people. To think, it all begins with the fear caused by this spirit.

Can you see where it comes from and how it works? If we can be made afraid, get impatient, become self-willed, prideful, disobedient, and act foolishly, we will cause others distress and trouble. Then, my friend, we're on our way to hurt God's church and His people. The road of destruction is being paved with this King Saul spirit, and it's using us to destroy other children of God.

Listen to this story. There was Rob, a handsome young man, very humble. He was born-again, attending church every time the doors opened. He had an anointing on his life. He had a powerful voice and could sing like few others. Everyone knew that he was going to be the praise and worship leader some day. God had chosen him and anointed him with a fantastic voice and the ability to lead the worship. He was baptized with the Holy Spirit and had a heart for God and for the things of God. He sang prophetically many times in the worship service. Everyone loved Rob. He never spoke badly of anyone, always wanting to pray with you and help you wherever he could. Oh yes, he must have had his faults, like the rest of us. Still, he was an example to the entire congregation. What happened next was a surprise to everyone. No one would have expected it to happen to Rob . . . maybe someone else, but not Rob. You see, the problem was that Rob was still a young man. He had just graduated, and the church had an older man leading worship on Sundays. Rob sang specials and sometimes would lead worship on a Sunday or Wednesday evening when Brother James, the praise and worship leader, was out of town. Rob and the people knew it was a matter of time before Brother James would retire and make way for him. But Rob was young, and the pastor was not just going to put him into the position without knowing his plans for the future. Rob did not know this and started worrying why he was not being given the job as worship leader. Still, Rob was a good man and just went about his daily routine of going to work and coming home. After some time, however, the King Saul spirit showed up.

This is where all the trouble started. Rob became afraid after some time, when it started to look like Brother James was not going to give up his position as worship leader. As a matter of fact, it seemed like the pastor was not going to use Rob as a replacement for Brother James. **Fear** started manifesting in Rob's life. He became afraid that he would never be the new worship leader in the church. It seemed like the enemy was going to steal his opportunity to fulfill his dream. We must realize that this was a lie from the devil. The pastor was just waiting for the right time, and he had told Rob previously that the time would come. Rob just had to keep on doing what he was doing, and when the time was right, he would become the new, full-time worship leader of Faith Fellowship Church. No one expected the King Saul spirit to show up, because no one knew about it.

So after attacking Rob with fear, this demonic spirit made him **impatient**. Whenever he was on stage, standing in for Brother James, Rob started to take over the whole worship team, as if he had been appointed as the full-time worship leader already. He started being **self-willed**. He started suggesting, sometimes even demanding, that the team make changes in their dress and the arrangements to the music. He became **prideful** and spoke evil about Brother James. He told everyone Brother James was out of date, old-fashioned, and that he, Rob, could do better. **Disobedience** crept in, and he began to try to take over, **acting foolishly**, doing things his own way, and going over the head of his superiors. Rob went so far as to tell the team and the church people that he thought the time had come for him to be chosen as the new worship leader. He started to **distress** the people around him with his demands and accusations, **troubling** everyone he talked to about this situation. When people saw Rob coming, they would get distressed, knowing what Rob was going to talk about. He was going to speak evil and criticize and be prideful. This troubled many people, and they did not know what to do to handle the situation. They did not want to go talk to the pastor or Brother James and get Rob into trouble. They all knew that Rob was to be appointed soon.

Some of the people agreed with him when he criticized Brother James. They also attacked some of the musicians and the pastor, who was taking too long to make the change. This made the people, who sided with him, sin as well. Rob—the chosen, anointed, Holy Ghost-filled man of God, born-again, and humble—had changed. He was not the same guy he used to be. He did not care if Brother James was getting hurt or not. Brother James could have gotten offended and backslid. Rob was just fighting for himself. No more mister nice guy. Why? Well, the King Saul spirit had shown up and was starting a path of destruction, as you will see . . . to be continued!

Summary of this chapter: Did you recognize all the characteristics of the attack of the King Saul spirit on Rob's life? There was the fear, impatience, self-will, pride, disobedience, foolishness, and distressing and troubling the other people. That's right, my friend, Rob could be you or me, the churchgoing member, maybe in another situation. It could be a pastor, the worship leader, a Sunday school teacher, or even a deacon or board member. It could be the normal churchgoing Christian, you and me. This King Saul spirit is on the move, and it's attacking us. These same characteristics are still being used, thousands of years after King Saul was attacked and destroyed, and it's still destroying churches and people.

Let's look at the next characteristic of this King Saul spirit.

CHAPTER 8

The Change in King Saul

REBELLION, LYING, AND ACCUSING

———〰———

King Saul was so affected and deceived by the King Saul spirit that he just could not change for the good. After he first let fear decide his actions, impatience, self-will, disobedience, pride, and foolishness followed. Soon King Saul's life went further awry. This King Saul spirit does not play games. When it starts working, it doesn't let go or give up. Its whole motive is to kill and destroy everything and everyone in its way.

King Saul had messed up, but God could still use him. So Samuel went to King Saul and gave him a mission to accomplish. God wanted King Saul to attack Amalek and utterly destroy everything and every one of them.

Now go and <u>attack Amalek,</u> and utterly <u>destroy all that they have,</u> and do not spare them. But <u>kill both man and woman, infant and nursing child, ox and sheep, camel and donkey.</u>
— 1 Samuel 15:3, (emphasis mine)

However, King Saul listened to the King Saul spirit again. He did not do what God had commanded him to do. He was disobedient again and **rebelled** against God. He did not kill Agag, the king of Amalek, nor did he kill all the animals. He kept some of the good ones and only destroyed the worthless animals.

He also took Agag king of the Amalekites alive, and utterly destroyed all the people with the edge of the sword. But Saul and the people <u>spared Agag and the best of the sheep, the oxen, the fatlings, the lambs,</u> and all that was good, and were unwilling to utterly destroy them. But everything despised and worthless, that they utterly destroyed.
— 1 Samuel 15:8-9, (emphasis mine)

King Saul did not perform God's commandment. So God sent Samuel to King Saul again. Guess what? When Samuel confronted King Saul, a new characteristic showed up: **lying.** Saul lied to Samuel as if he had done everything God had asked of him.

Then Samuel went to Saul, and Saul said to him, "Blessed are you of the Lord! I have

performed the commandment of the Lord."
But Samuel said, "What then is this bleating
of the sheep in my ears, and the lowing of the
oxen which I hear?"

—1 Samuel 15:13-14

What a disgrace, lying bluntly to a man of God.
So when Samuel asked Saul about the animals that
were still alive, the king turned around and **accused**
the people. He said that the people needed the animals
to sacrifice to God.

And Saul said, "They have brought them from
the Amalekites; for the people spared the best
of the sheep and the oxen, to sacrifice to the
Lord your God; and the rest we have utterly
destroyed."

—1 Samuel 15:15

Well, Samuel did not spare King Saul for his
stupidity, as we read in **1 Samuel 15:16-19.**

Samuel told King Saul to keep quiet, to shut his
mouth and say no more. I think the prophet had had
it with King Saul by then. Samuel then took King
Saul back to the beginning of his journey as king. He
reminded Saul of the man he once had been. Samuel
told him that he had not obeyed God and had done
evil. See how Saul answered Samuel:

And Saul said to Samuel, "But I have obeyed
the voice of the Lord, and gone on the mission
on which the Lord sent me, and brought

back Agag king of Amalek; I have utterly destroyed the Amalekites. But the people took of the plunder, sheep and oxen, the best of the things which should have been utterly destroyed, to sacrifice to the Lord your God in Gilgal."

— 1 Samuel 15:20-21

Saul, still deceived by the King Saul spirit, lied again. He accused the people of taking the spoil. What a coward. Then he used *the need to sacrifice to God* as an excuse. Can you see how sly this King Saul spirit is? Samuel's answer was devastating.

So Samuel said: "Has the Lord as great delight in burnt offerings and sacrifices, as in obeying the voice of the Lord? Behold, to obey is better than sacrifice, and to heed than the fat of rams. For rebellion is as the sin of witchcraft, and stubbornness is as iniquity and idolatry. Because you have rejected the word of the Lord, He also has rejected you from being king."

— 1 Samuel 15:22-23

"King Saul, over and above of being a **liar** and an **accuser**, you are also in **rebellion**," Samuel told King Saul. He also reminded King Saul that the sin of rebellion was as the sin of witchcraft. Saul had rejected God's Word. This was serious, my friend.

You see, the King Saul spirit is doing exactly the same thing in our churches today. It's attacking the

Christians with rebellion, or disobedience, with lying and accusation.

Just look at the born-again children of God today. Are they all obedient? Or are some in rebellion, rejecting God's Word like King Saul did? People are not following God's Word. They are not paying tithes; they do not love and forgive, as instructed in the Word. Hate is everywhere, even in the church. I'm not talking about the people that don't believe in God; no, I'm talking about Christians. Look how they're hurting their brothers and sisters in Christ. Disagreeing, fighting, splitting up churches, and badmouthing their pastors, even getting them fired. It's common practice nowadays. They're trying to do it their way and not God's way. Spiritual witchcraft, rejection of God's Word, rebellion, and disobedience are keeping the modern church busy. Let me remind you: God does not like it, and He won't stand for it. He never has and never will.

The problem is we have a church full of lying people, too. They will lie about things when you confront them and give other people the blame. It's funny that it's never them, always someone else. Come on, you all know what I'm talking about. Just look at the promises people are making and never keeping; we call that lying. "Well I could not . . ." and then the excuses come. How many people have messages on their cell phones that say, *"Please leave your name and number and a short message, and I* **will** *call you back* **as soon as possible."** If you make these promises, why don't you keep them? Well, Hansie, is that really a lie? What is lying, then? If you said you'd call back soon, do it, or else you're lying. If you say you'll do something and you don't do it, it's a lie. It's the opposite of the truth, as easy as that.

Are there no excuses allowed? Well, of course there are. All of us have things happen to us, and we can't always do what we said we would do, immediately. You can still make it right later on, and then give your excuse. I've been busy some days, and I could only call back the next day. At least I called and said I was sorry for the inconvenience. I don't want to be a liar. I've been around people who, when they saw the number on their caller ID, would say, "Oh no, man, not that guy again. I'm not even going to answer or call him back." Hallo, your answering machine said you'd call him back! Rather, answer the phone and tell the man, in a loving, serious way, not to call again, that you're not interested. It takes away the opportunity to have to lie.

We have to get to the point where we realize that this King Saul spirit is attacking the church and Christians. And the Christians are **accusing** each other of being the problem, instead of recognizing that the problem is the King Saul spirit.

Remember our friend Rob, the good, young upcoming worship leader? Well, let's pick up his story and see what happened next.

The previous chapter told us that Rob was so full of fear of not getting the job as worship leader that he got impatient and self-willed. He became disobedient, taking matters into his own hands. His increased pride caused him to act foolishly. He started speaking evil and distressed and troubled many of the people in the church. He drew others in as partners in his sin.

Well, the pastor saw the warning signs and went to Rob and ministered to him. The pastor told him how to handle this situation according to the Word of God. He told Rob what God expected of him and what the Word said about his sin. Rob had to go make right with everyone and tell them he was wrong and apologize. The pastor encouraged Rob again to wait for the right time for him to be appointed as the new worship leader. He also had to forgive everyone and ask God's forgiveness. Rob had God's Word spoken to him, and he knew what to do. Rob agreed, and everything looked like it was going to work out. Nobody knew that the King Saul spirit was still around, having only just begun its destroying work.

The next week came and Rob did nothing. The following week came and still no change in Rob. As a matter of fact, Brother James had to leave town again, and Rob was taking charge again. He acted as if the pastor had not said anything to him. Well, you know what happened next, right? The pastor heard about the lingering situation and called Rob in. He told Rob that he was in **rebellion** to authority and being **disobedient** to God's Word. The pastor wanted to know why he had not sorted out the situation and why he was still doing exactly what he had done before. This is when the trouble escalated. Rob answered according to the King Saul spirit. He started **lying.** He actually told the pastor that he had asked for forgiveness. He said he had made right with Brother James and had done all that the pastor had asked him to do. We all know he was lying. Rob had not done any of these things. Rob was busy with witchcraft. He had rejected what his pastor had told him, and what God wanted him to do. Rob had rejected God's Word. He was lying to the pastor about the whole situation.

The pastor asked him about his controlling attitude over the worship team. He wanted to know why the same accusations were still being made and why Brother James was still the target of evil talk and criticism from the worship team. Do you know what Rob said? You guessed it. He actually told the pastor that it was the worship team members that did not like Brother James. The team allegedly wanted him out. They wanted Rob to be the leader, because Rob was far better than Brother James. He said that there were people in the congregation that were spreading the rumors that Rob was a much better singer and leader than Brother James. The people wanted him in and Brother James out. He said the people could not understand why the pastor did not let Brother James go and let him, Rob, be the worship leader. He **accused others** of being the bad guys, while he supposedly did nothing wrong. It sounds just like King Saul, doesn't it? Well, it is, because the same spirit was in control of both of them, the King Saul spirit.

Summary of this chapter: Saul—a chosen, anointed man of God, who had the Holy Spirit on him and could prophesy, having God with him— changed into another man, a different man with a new heart. This humble, peaceful king turned into an evil man, all because of the King Saul spirit. He became fearful, impatient, disobedient, prideful, self-willed, and acted foolishly in God's eyes. He became rebellious, openly lying and accusing his own people of doing the wrong, while he, King Saul, made himself innocent. This is how many in the church are acting, today. We're allowing this King Saul spirit to attack us and destroy us, just like he had attacked and destroyed King Saul. By the time a person is in rebellion toward God, openly lying and accusing others, they've got a lot of problems. If this is where the story ended, we could still do something about it and change it, but unfortunately it gets worse.

The next characteristic of the King Saul spirit caused serious problems.

CHAPTER 9

The Serious Change in King Saul

THE HOLY SPIRIT DEPARTS

—︎∽∾︎—

My dear friend, unfortunately, up to this point we have only seen and heard of the mild characteristics of the King Saul spirit. After causing King Saul to rebel, lie, and accuse his own people falsely, the serious change in King Saul began taking place. Then, the real destruction started.

Let's go back to **1 Samuel 15:24-30.** After Samuel told Saul that he was in **rebellion,** or witchcraft, and that God had rejected him as king because he had rejected the Word of God, King Saul confessed his sin to Samuel. He realized that being full of fear, impatient, prideful, self-willed, disobedient, and foolish was sin. He knew that distressing the people with his rebellion, lies, and accusations was wrong.

The problem was that he did **not repent**. He had confessed that he had sinned, but he didn't repent to God. He asked Samuel to forgive him, but not God. Samuel told King Saul that it was basically too late. God had rejected King Saul. He made him understand that the kingship was going to be taken away from him and given to someone else. What a price to pay! To have all these good qualities as a king and lose them all! It's not worth it, my friend.

> Then <u>Saul said to Samuel</u>, "<u>I have sinned</u>, for I have transgressed the commandment of the Lord and your words, because I feared the people and obeyed their voice. Now therefore, <u>please pardon my sin</u>, and return with me, that I may worship the Lord." But Samuel said to Saul, "I will not return with you, for you have rejected the word of the Lord, and <u>the Lord has rejected you from being king over Israel.</u>" And as Samuel turned around to go away, Saul seized the edge of his robe, and it tore. So Samuel said to him, "The Lord has torn the kingdom of Israel from you today, and has given it to a neighbor of yours, who is better than you."
> —1 Samuel 15:24-28, (emphasis mine)

So what happened next? Well, Samuel had to go and finish the job to kill Agag, whom Saul should have killed.

Now let's look at a very important point. King Saul had made all these mistakes, and had sinned big time, but he still wanted to worship God, apart from all the wrong he did. If you listen to him, it sounded like he was still interested in serving God, and in a way he was.

> Then he said, "I have sinned; yet honor me now, please, before the elders of my people and before Israel, and return with me, that I may worship the Lord your God." So Samuel turned back after Saul, and Saul worshiped the Lord.
>
> —1 Samuel 15:30-31

People who are attacked by the King Saul spirit still want to worship and serve God. The problem is, it's not so easy at this point in their Christian lives because of their relationship with God that's not where it should be.

God kept King Saul from reigning over Israel. He was sorry that He had made him king. **1 Samuel 15:11:** *"I greatly regret that I have set up Saul as king, for he has turned back from following Me, and has not performed My commandments."* Another Scripture states; **1Samuel 16:1:** *"Now the LORD said to Samuel, "How long will you mourn for Saul, seeing I have rejected him from reigning over Israel?"*

So God sent Samuel to go anoint the new king of Israel. You all know who that was, right? Samuel had to go to Jesse and, after looking at all of his sons, eventually chose the shepherd boy, David. Samuel anointed David to be the next king over Israel (**1 Sam. 16:1-13).** The only problem was that King Saul had not yet been removed from the office of king.

Well, God knew the exact time that He was going to remove King Saul and replace him with David. So now we have the current king, King Saul, and a new king in waiting.

I want to remind you that King Saul knew this. Remember that he was told by Samuel that God had rejected him as king and was going to replace him **(1 Sam. 15:26-28)**. Samuel actually told him it was going to be a neighbor. That must have started a reaction in King Saul's mind: *"Who was it going to be?"* He had no clue that it would be David.

Nevertheless, God was still going to use King Saul on the battlefield. He was still going to give him victories, for the sake of His people, Israel. Unfortunately for King Saul, the continual willful sin in his life caused the **Holy Spirit to depart** from him. This opened the door to a distressing evil spirit, which replaced the Holy Spirit. Oh my, what a sad day in a person's life when that happens! No more Holy Spirit help, or comfort, or advice. He only had his own natural strength and ability to work with. Now King Saul was really in trouble. God was not with him anymore. He was on his own.

> But the <u>Spirit of the Lord departed from Saul,</u> and a distressing spirit from the Lord troubled him. And Saul's servants said to him, "Surely, a distressing spirit from God is troubling you."
>
> —1 Samuel 16:14-15, (emphasis mine)

As you read in the scripture above, God gave King Saul over to an evil spirit, a distressing spirit. God did not give him an evil spirit. God doesn't do those kinds of things. God only gives the Holy Spirit. He allowed the evil distressing spirit to attack King Saul. When we don't have the Holy Spirit with us, we're open to attack from evil spirits. That's just how it works. We then have no more protection from God, and any demonic spirit can attack us, control us, and use us.

So here we have King Saul, the anointed, chosen man of God, but without the Holy Spirit to help and comfort him: a king being tormented by a distressing, evil spirit. He was in a backslidden position. He needed help. Some of King Saul's servants suggested that he find a man with music skills, who could play the harp to him every time the evil spirit attacked. They believed this would calm him down and make him well. One of the servants said they knew of such a man, and that's how David ended up playing the harp to King Saul. So every time King Saul got tormented by this spirit, David would play and sing to him; the king would be refreshed, and the distressing evil spirit would leave him.

Do you see the difference between Saul and David? Both of them were anointed by God. The only difference was that King Saul was unable to repent, and so was without the Holy Spirit, backslidden. David, on the other hand, still had the Holy Spirit with him, serving God. That's why the evil spirit tormenting King Saul did not leave him until David showed up, full of the Holy Spirit. That's when the distressing spirit had to leave because the Holy Spirit was in the place. So it's clear to see that we can't afford to be without the Holy Spirit. Every evil spirit has to go when we're walking with the Spirit of God. Or else, like King Saul, we can be tormented by them.

> And Saul's servants said to him, "Surely, <u>a distressing spirit from God is troubling you.</u> Let our master now command your servants, who are before you, to seek out a man who is a skillful player on the harp; and it shall be that he will play it with his hand when the distressing spirit from God is upon you, and you shall be well." So Saul said to his servants, "Provide me now a man who can play well, and bring him to me." Then one of the servants answered and said, "Look, I have seen a son of Jesse the Bethlehemite, who is skillful in playing, a mighty man of valor, a man of war, prudent in speech, and a handsome person; and the Lord is with him." Therefore Saul sent messengers to Jesse, and said, "Send me your son David, who is with the sheep." So David came to Saul and stood before him. And he loved him greatly, and he became his armorbearer. Then Saul sent to Jesse, saying, "Please let David stand before me, for he has found favor in my sight." And so it was, whenever <u>the spirit from God was upon Saul,</u> that David would take a harp and play it with his hand. <u>Then Saul would become</u>

refreshed and well, and the distressing spirit
would depart from him.
    — 1 Samuel 16:15-18, (emphasis mine)

David, however, was not just any young boy
anymore. He was anointed to be the next king. Now
he was playing the harp to the man he was going to
replace. Saul did not yet know that David was going
to be his replacement. So he loved him and made
him his armor bearer. King Saul loved David, and so
did Jonathan, King Saul's son. It all looked good for
David and King Saul. David was a great help to King
Saul when he was in distress, and he had the favor of
the king.

Well, I believe you all remember the next story,
so let me just go over it quickly. The Philistines
showed up and wanted to make war again. So Israel
had to go to war with them. They all assembled to
fight in the valley of Elah. Israel camped out on
one mountain and the Philistines on the other, with
the valley between them, waiting to start the battle.
The Philistines, however, had a big powerful giant,
Goliath, who came forward and challenged King
Saul to send out a man to fight him. Whoever won
the battle with Goliath would win the battle between
the two nations. The only difficulty was that Israel
had no one big enough or strong enough to go and
fight this giant. Every day Goliath would come and
speak evil over Israel and their God, but no one was
brave enough to go and fight him. They were all too
afraid. They just sat and waited for something to
happen. The whole of Israel, along with their king,

became cowards. Once again, they could not believe that God would help them.

> And the Philistine said, "I defy the armies of Israel this day; give me a man, that we may fight together." When Saul and all Israel heard these words of the Philistine, they were dismayed and greatly afraid. . . . And the Philistine drew near and presented himself forty days, morning and evening.
> — 1 Samuel 17:10-11, 16

David had three brothers in the army, and he had to go give them some supplies from their father, Jesse. When David got to the battlefield and heard Goliath speak, he became so angry that he told King Saul he would go fight the giant. You all know how King Saul tried to stop him. David's brothers tried to stop him, too, but David said that God was with him and he could kill the giant. After trying on King Saul's heavy armor in vain, David decided to make use of his own weapons to go kill Goliath. He reminded King Saul that he had killed lions and bears before; God had helped him then, and He would help him again against this Philistine. David told them that he did not need a sword or any armor. He just went with a sling, five round stones, and his God.

I can imagine the king and the brothers thinking, *"What a waste, that a young man should die. What stupidity."* Well, they couldn't stop David. Remember, he had the Holy Spirit, and King Saul didn't. David got to the valley, met his enemy, and after some famous words between the two of them, David slung the stone and struck the giant in his forehead. Goliath fell to the ground and was dead. David took the giant's sword and cut off his head, taking it back to King Saul. David became a hero that day. King Saul set him over all the men of war from that day on. He sent him everywhere to fight and make war. David and Jonathan became very close, too, and made a covenant with each other. All the servants and men of King Saul accepted David. David became a successful warrior, respected by everyone, having favor with the people and the king.

However, problems started when King Saul became worried that David was doing too well. The people were starting to compare the two of them, especially in songs about their battle victories.

Now it had happened as they were coming home, when David was returning from the slaughter of the Philistine, that the women had come out of all the cities of Israel, singing and dancing, to meet King Saul, with tambourines, with joy, and with musical instruments. So the women sang as they danced, and said: "Saul has slain his thousands, And David his ten thousands."

—1 Samuel 18:6-7, (emphasis mine)

This became dangerous for David.

I think I need to relate this whole sad episode of King Saul, being oppressed by an evil spirit, to our lives, right now. When we're in continual willful sin, like King Saul, the Holy Spirit can depart from us, too. Why? Well, because many Christians can sin willfully, but never repent of these sins. King Saul did the same thing. Without the Holy Spirit, who is our Anointer, we can do nothing.

I believe that's why we have Christians in church, who appear to be serving God, but have lost the Holy Spirit. You can find them. They are distressed, oppressed, and unhappy people, with no joy: miserable people. Oh, they look like they're doing fine, but if you could only see the real true person on the inside, being tormented by this King Saul spirit! This is when we as Christians can open the door to more dangerous demonic spirits, who can attack us and harm us. If you allow the King Saul spirit to get you to the place where the Holy Spirit departs from you, you're on your own. Not a good place to be. Can the Holy Spirit depart from a Christian? Of course He can. If a Christian does not want to serve God no more, he can backslide and want nothing to do with the Holy Spirit. We can quench the Holy Spirit, or put Him out, extinguish Him, stop Him, resist Him. **1 Thessalonians 5:19;** *Do not quench the Spirit.* When a Christian backslides he is back in the world. At that point in his life the Holy Spirit means nothing to him, it's foolishness to the natural person. **1 Corinthians 2:14;** *But the natural man does not receive the things of the Spirit of God, for they are foolishness to him; nor can he know them, because they are spiritually discerned.* So the answer is yes, the Holy Spirit can depart from you and me, if we allow Him too.

Summary of this chapter: When a born-again child of God, chosen and anointed, loses the Holy Spirit, there are serious problems. We cannot function without the Holy Spirit, and the enemy knows that. That's why the devil would like to get us to the point where we are so influenced and controlled by the King Saul spirit that the Holy Spirit eventually departs from us. When does the Holy Spirit depart from a child of God? It could happen when people act like King Saul and stay in willful sin, refusing to repent.

In the following chapter, the King Saul spirit exposes its next characteristic: jealousy.

CHAPTER 10

The Serious Change in King Saul

JEALOUSY

—〰—

David helped King Saul, while he was playing the harp and singing songs. The moment David started becoming more famous and well-liked than King Saul, the next characteristic of the King Saul spirit surfaced: you guessed right, **jealousy**. King Saul got angry, frustrated, displeased, and annoyed. He became jealous and suspicious of David.

> Then Saul was very angry, and the saying displeased him; and he said, "They have ascribed to David ten thousands, and to me they have ascribed only thousands. Now what more can he have but the kingdom?" So Saul eyed David from that day forward.
> —1 Samuel 18:8-9, (emphasis mine)

When you become jealous of someone, you can't really like that person anymore. You think that the other person is doing better than you are doing, right? People start comparing themselves to one another. Envy enters, and if you don't watch out, jealousy can lead to serious trouble. Remember Joseph? His brothers became jealous of him because he had dreams of them bowing before him. They were so jealous that they wanted to kill him. So they threw Joseph in the pit. Before they could kill him, slave traders came by, and the brothers traded him for money. The fact is that their jealousy drove them to the point where they would kill. Well, that's what this King Saul spirit did. It drove King Saul to become so jealous of David that he wanted to kill him. Remember what I said in the beginning of the book. The King Saul spirit is a destroying spirit. It wants to kill. It's actually a killing spirit. So jealousy can lead to murder. What are we going to do about it? If we keep on entertaining jealousy in our lives, we can end up killers, physically or spiritually.

Let's look at Rob again. You remember his rebellion and disobedience to his pastor's suggestions. Then he lied to the pastor and accused the people of speaking evil and criticizing Brother James. Rob never repented, because he thought he was right and everyone else was wrong. The Holy Spirit departed from him. Oh, Rob was still a good leader with a good voice, but his anointing was gone, Rob was on his own. When Rob was on the stage leading praise and worship, there was pride, and you could feel it and see it. This opened the door for an evil distressing spirit to come and attack Rob.

The pastor still used Rob to fill in when Brother James was gone, because he hoped the man would repent and change. The young man had a calling from God, but he was messing it up. So the pastor had to start looking for someone to replace Brother James, and it was not going to be Rob. The pastor told Rob what he was planning to do, which not only made Rob furious and angry, but also jealous. He became jealous of anyone who could sing in the church. He knew he was not going to be the new worship leader anymore, but who was it going to be? This question tormented Rob. Instead of repenting and making right, Rob just allowed himself to be used by the King Saul spirit. Nevertheless, he had a good idea who his competition was going to be, because there was another guy who was being used as a stand-in for Brother James. Rob did not like the idea. The problem was when Thomas, the new guy, did the worship, it was anointed, and you could feel God moving again. This really helped the church and the team, because of the anointing on Thomas's life. Rob had an idea; he was going to stop this *"infiltration"* of Thomas. It looked liked the people were favoring Thomas more than they favored him. So Rob decided to do something to get Thomas out of the way. Rob thought maybe he could still have a chance at the worship leader position.

The King Saul spirit had begun its destruction. It was going to use Rob to destroy Thomas, to kill him spiritually. This spirit was going to use Rob to make

Thomas backslide. The spirit of murder came upon Rob. How does this happen? Well the Word says if you hate your brother you are a murderer **(1 John 3:15).** The King Saul spirit caused Rob to start hating Thomas, another chosen, anointed man of God. The murder plan was ready to be implemented . . . to be continued.

Why did the pastor not get rid of Rob? Sometimes we ministers make mistakes too, right? There are many people who don't discern this King Saul spirit. That includes pastors. I'm using Rob as the example, but pastors, you and I, or anyone else could be attacked by the King Saul spirit. The pastor never got rid of Rob, because he did not recognize the King Saul spirit. To be honest, he'd never even heard of it before, so how could he have done something about it?

He did what any good pastor would have done. He spoke with Rob, gave him direction, prayed with him, and counseled him several times. It did not work. The pastor should have let Rob go as soon as he had recognized the problem. But he did not discern the real problem, because he did not know the King Saul spirit existed. Only after Rob had confessed, repented, and made right with God, could he have been allowed back into the worship team. Rob had backslidden, but not even the pastor realized the reason behind his sin.

Many Christians are in this position today. They're chosen, anointed of God, have the Holy Spirit of God, are with God all the time, and are prophesying with new hearts. They're born-again children of God. These Christians are being attacked by the King Saul spirit; fear and impatience begin, followed by self-will, pride, and disobedience. They start acting foolishly and troubling others. Instead of confessing and repenting of their sins, they start rebelling against God's Word and any other form of authority. They lie to and accuse one another of being evil, and they think they're right. Does this sound familiar to you? This is when the Christian can lose his anointing, because the Holy Spirit departs. The born-again Christians, in church, without the Holy Spirit, are now controlled and bound up by an evil, distressing demon spirit. These are the Christians who are backslidden, and most of them don't even realize it. Then the jealousy starts and the destruction comes. Hatred is stirred up and the spirit of murder makes an appearance. The church is in trouble, because Christians are destroying Christians.

Now remember what I said in the beginning. Don't think about other people who are acting like this or have some of these characteristics. Let's look at our own lives. Are we acting like this? Are we being attacked by this King Saul spirit? It's time to take a good look at ourselves. It's time to judge our own spiritual lives. If we find out that this King Saul spirit is attacking and using us, we better repent; confess to God, and change. There is time to make it right, my friend. If you feel that you've *not been* used or attacked by this King Saul spirit yet, be careful; it's still out there. Remember we are more powerful than this King Saul spirit. We are overcomers, we can overcome it.

Summary of this chapter: The King Saul spirit does not have to go according to this sequence, starting with fear, impatience, and so forth, as we've seen in Rob or King Saul. It can start anywhere. You don't have to be afraid first. This King Saul spirit can use any of its characteristics. It can start with any one of them. It does not have to wait for you to get fearful to show up. No, it can attack you in any weak moment, when you're disobedient or jealous or even prideful. It will start wherever you allow it to start. Why? Well, because it's main aim is to kill and destroy. The sooner you get to the latter point, the better for the King Saul spirit. The sooner you can make your brother or sister in the Lord fall, backslide, cause a split in the church, or destroy someone's life, the better for this spirit.

So please understand this today. Anytime, anywhere, any of these characteristics of the King Saul spirit can show up and attack us. If we don't get the attack under control, we're going to come under control of the King Saul spirit. This will lead to a path of destruction in our lives, and we'll go the same way King Saul did. We'll be an instrument in the hands of this King Saul spirit, and we'll start destroying our fellow Christians and our churches. Let's look at how King Saul ended up murderous, wanting to kill David after he had become jealous of him.

CHAPTER 11

The Serious Change
in King Saul

THROWING SPEARS

—◆—

The **spirit of killing,** or **murder,** attacked King Saul, because he had developed hatred toward David. When you hate someone, you're the same as a murderer, you know.

> Whoever <u>hates his brother is a murderer,</u> and you know that no murderer has eternal life abiding in him.
> — 1 John 3:15, (emphasis mine)

King Saul still used David to play music for him when the distressing spirit came upon him, but with a difference. After he became jealous of David's victories over the enemy, he started hating David and developed murderous thoughts about him.

And it happened on the next day that the
distressing spirit from God came upon Saul,
and he prophesied inside the house. So David
played music with his hand, as at other times;
but there was <u>a spear</u> in Saul's hand. And Saul
<u>cast the spear,</u> for he said, "<u>I will pin David
to the wall!</u>" But David escaped his presence
twice.

      —1 Samuel 18:10-11, (emphasis mine)

King Saul still let David play and sing to him, but
he had already made up his mind to kill him. He was
listening to David with a spear in his hand. David,
of course, was not expecting this kind of treatment
from the man who had loved him and favored him
before. One day, while David played on his harp,
King Saul threw the spear at David, to kill him. The
only reason David was not killed was because God
was with him and had already chosen him to be the
follow-up to King Saul. So David escaped, and King
Saul became even more afraid of David. Recognize
that fear again?

Now Saul was <u>afraid of David</u>, because the
Lord was with him, <u>but had departed from
Saul.</u>

      —1 Samuel 18:12, (emphasis mine)

You see, a man of God should not want to spear
his brothers or sisters to the wall. The only time you
would want to do that is when the Holy Spirit is not
with you. A Holy Ghost-filled person should not do

such a thing to his neighbors. We're supposed to love our neighbors, not kill them. Most of the times people who have backslidden, like King Saul, entertain these thoughts. He actually tried to kill David *twenty-one times*. Can you believe it? I know some people are thinking, *"Why did God not forgive King Saul and help him?"* Well, he never repented of his sin. *"What about God's mercy?"* you would ask. *"Where was that?"* It wasn't there, for the reason that God had removed His mercy from King Saul, as well as His Holy Spirit. In the next verse, God explains that He wouldn't take away His mercy from David, as He took it away from Saul.

> But My <u>mercy</u> shall not depart from [David], <u>as I took it from Saul,</u> whom I removed from before you.
> —2 Samuel 7:15, (emphasis mine)

No Holy Spirit, no mercy. King Saul had no one to help him; he was on his own.

Twenty-one times King Saul tried to kill David, or have him murdered. This is what this King Saul spirit does the best: killing, hurting people and destroying churches.

Let me explain this killing spree of King Saul.

Three times King Saul tried to kill David with a spear (**1 Sam. 18:11, twice; 1 Sam. 19:8-10, once**).

One time by scheming to have him killed by the Philistines (**1 Sam. 18:17-19**).

One time through Michal his wife and the Philistines **(1 Sam. 18:20-30).**

One time by trying to get Jonathan, his own son, and all his own servants to kill him **(1 Sam. 19:1-7).**

Two times by sending messengers to David's house **(1 Sam. 19:11-14-16).**

Three times by sending messengers to Ramah **(1 Sam. 19:17-21).**

One time by personally going to Ramah **(1 Sam. 19:22-24).**

Two times by planning to kill him at the feast **(1 Sam. 20:24-30).**

One time by commanding that he be brought from home to die **(1 Sam. 20:31-42).**

One time making war on Keilah to kill David **(1 Sam. 23:8-13).**

One time seeking him in the wilderness of Ziph **(1 Sam. 23:14-18).**

One time by sending spies to find him and kill him **(1 Sam. 23:19-24).**

One time by sending his army after him to kill him **(1 Sam. 23:25-29).**

One time by going after David himself, with three thousand selected men, but falling into David's hands and his life being spared **(1 Sam. 24:1-22).**

One time again going after David with a selected army, but falling into his hands a second time and being spared **(1 Sam. 26:1-25).**

Not one of these attempts was successful. God helped David escape every time the attacks came. This King Saul spirit wanted David dead and had done everything possible to kill him.

The King Saul spirit even used King Saul to kill the priests of God. This spirit did not spare anyone. It went after David, and anyone who got in its way was killed as well. Doeg the Edomite, who was set over the servants of King Saul, had heard where David had escaped and who had helped him. So they all set off to the city of Nob, where they found the priest Ahimelech. The other priests with him came forward as well. Then King Saul asked them why they had helped David. Well, what a dumb question to ask! Ahimelech told the king that he helped David because he was his son-in-law. King Saul did not like this answer. He did not want people helping David escape, so he commanded his guards to kill all the priests. They did not want to touch the priests, so King Saul told Doeg to kill them all. Doeg killed every one of them, even their wives and children. The whole city was murdered because of this evil King Saul spirit.

> Then the king said to the guards who stood about him, "Turn and kill the priests of the Lord, because their hand also is with David, and because they knew when he fled and did not tell it to me." But the servants of the king would not lift their hands to strike the priests of the Lord. And the king said to Doeg, "You turn and kill the priests!" So Doeg

the Edomite turned and struck the priests, and killed on that day eighty-five men who wore a linen ephod. Also Nob, the city of the priests, he struck with the edge of the sword, both men and women, children and nursing infants, oxen and donkeys and sheep—with the edge of the sword.

—1 Samuel 22:17-19

This was a great slaughter of the priests and all their families. This killing spirit had no mercy at all.

While all these attempts were being made to kill David, King Saul was still king, remember? Unfortunately, the Holy Spirit had departed from him, and he had lost his anointing. King Saul had backslidden. He was not serving God like he should. So the lying spirit surfaced again. Saul promised to stop the killing spree; he even swore to his son Jonathan that he would not kill David.

So Saul heeded the voice of Jonathan, <u>and Saul swore, "As the Lord lives, he shall not be killed."</u>

—1 Samuel 19:6, (emphasis mine)

What a lie! It wasn't long after that when Saul tried to pin David to the wall with the spear again. You could not depend on King Saul's word. He would say one thing and do another. He was lying all the time. While following David and seeking to kill him, King Saul got so angry that he even forced David's wife, Michal, to marry another man. This was wicked. He would do anything to destroy David. Well, destruction is what this King Saul spirit wants.

> But Saul had given Michal his daughter,
> David's wife, to Palti the son of Laish, who
> was from Gallim.
>
> — 1 Samuel 25:44

How can you just decide to give your married daughter away to another man? Well, you have to be so controlled by the King Saul spirit that you want to destroy everyone and everything around you.

What about us? Are we busy murdering our fellow Christians, like King Saul wanted to kill David? There are many born-again Christians in church, who started off so well in their Christian life, growing spiritually. Somewhere along the path they allowed this King Saul spirit to take control of their lives. Let me ask you the question like this: *"How many spears have you and I thrown, and how many of our fellow Christians are pinned to the church's walls?"* If we could see in the spiritual realm, I wonder how many skeletons we would see hanging on the wall of our churches. How many Christians, are killed by fellow Christians, by thrown spears.

Christians, born-again, in the church, but bound up and controlled by the King Saul spirit, are busy spearing fellow Christians sitting next to them in the pews. How? Well let's identify some spears. What about the spear of gossip, the spear of criticism, the spear of judgment? What about the spear of hatred, the spear of bitterness, the spear of unforgiveness?

How many spears have been thrown by slandering people and putting them in a bad light: accusing them falsely, speaking negatively about them, and breaking down their character? How many spears of jealousy, of hurt, and of harm have been thrown? How many spears of cruelty have been thrown? Are you with me? Are you getting the point? The church is full of it, and no one can deny it. You know as well as I do that it's the truth.

The problem is that the person we're attempting to spear is a chosen, anointed by God, born-again Christian, sitting next to us in church. The anointed of God is spearing the other anointed of God. How crazy! Are we allowed to hurt and spear God's anointed? No, of course we're not. God said in **Psalm 105:15:** *"Do not touch My anointed, and do My prophets no harm."* So how dare we try and kill our anointed brothers and sisters with these spears? How dare we harm them? Well, once again, it's done through the King Saul spirit, when we allow it to attack and use us.

Some of you might even be thinking that you're definitely not anointed by God. I've got news for you, my friend. Every born-again child of God is anointed.

> But you have an anointing from the Holy One, and you know all things.
>
> —1 John 2:20

> But <u>the anointing which you have received from Him abides in you,</u> and you do not

need that anyone teach you; but as the same anointing teaches you concerning all things, and is true, <u>and is not a lie,</u> and just as it has taught you, you will abide in Him.

— 1 John 2:27, (emphasis mine)

You see, friend, you have been anointed, and the Word says that the anointing abides in you, which is not a lie. The word, *abide* means "to stay in you, to remain in you, dwell in you, to be present in you." But when the Holy Spirit departs, and the Christian backslides, that's when things change. That's the work of the King Saul spirit.

That's when love makes room for hate. That's when the destroying characteristics surface. That's when Christians, who you never thought would harm you, start throwing these spears at you: all for their own gain, they try to kill or murder you, spiritually. I know this sounds harsh, but this is what's happening in our churches, and we'll have to deal with it, or give in to it and perish.

I'm going to repeat this again. This King Saul spirit wants you out of the church. It wants you to leave the church. This spirit will split the church to get what it wants. It will use us to kill and destroy each other. The sad news is it uses normal Christians like you and me to do its dirty work. At the same time, this King Saul spirit is hurting the one it's attacking as well. Not only the other person. We'll get to this important point a bit later on.

How are we affected? A lot of Christians have died spiritually because of the treatment they got in church. They were so hurt and harmed through other born-again Christians throwing spears that they left the church and never came back. They stopped serving God because of the spearing of fellow Christians, and then they backslid. Why? Well, nobody expects the spearing to come from brothers and sisters in the Lord, do they? Welcome to the real world, my friend. No wonder the church is in such a mess. No one wants to address these issues. Hoping the problems will go away just does not work. God will keep us accountable for the losses of His precious saints. One day, we will give full account of every Christian we have speared. It's not our job to gossip, judge, or criticize our anointed brothers or sisters sitting in the pew next to us. God never told us to do these things. It seems like we're just ignoring the Word from God, spearing whomever we can. This is happening in our churches. Churches split and people leave because they are offended by other Christians. Somewhere we'll have to stop this behavior.

The example of Rob looks more and more like King Saul and David's situation. Let's look at Rob's story again. Rob had done wrong. He became afraid, impatient, disobedient, and prideful. He became self-willed, disobedient, and foolish. Then he got the people involved in his scheme and troubled and distressed them. When the pastor approached him and asked him to make things right, Rob did not repent, but lied to the pastor and accused the other members of the worship team of doing wrong. He rejected God's Word and his pastor's advice. He became rebellious. Rob lost his relationship with God, and he backslid.

He had lost his anointing. The Holy Spirit was not with him anymore; He had departed from him.

God told the pastor to look for another anointed man to do the worship when Brother James was not available. This made Rob so angry, and he became very jealous of the new guy, Thomas. So Rob decided to get rid of Thomas. The only way to do this was to discredit Thomas so much that the people would not accept him as Brother James's replacement. Rob started throwing spears of criticism, spears of gossip, and false accusation toward Thomas. He spoke evil of Thomas everywhere he went. He told everyone Thomas's mistakes and supposed shortcomings. The spears just kept flying. He even tried to look into Thomas's past life to find out if he had been divorced. Maybe he could find out if Thomas had used drugs and smoked or abused alcohol. Rob tried to destroy Thomas and discredit the man by using anything and anyone he could find. His motive was to murder this man spiritually so that he would leave the church or backslide. As long as he could get Thomas out of the way, things would be good for Rob. You see, Rob wanted Thomas "spiritually dead" . . . destroyed.

You can imagine what the atmosphere in the church was like. One man of God was trying to destroy another man of God. If that wasn't enough, the other members of the church also were involved in this battle. There was a spirit of disagreement between the people. There were the ones who liked Rob, and the ones who liked Thomas and Brother James. The pastor, on the other hand, was in the middle, trying to be a good shepherd. He was trying to calm everyone down and explain what was going on. If only the pastor could see what this King Saul spirit was busy doing, then he could have stopped it right there in its tracks. However, slowly, very slowly, this King Saul spirit was busy splitting up the church, and no one had realized it or seen it coming. Well, what happened next? We'll soon find out!

Summary of this chapter: I hope you can recognize some of these characteristics in your own life or in the lives of other Christians in your church. With more knowledge of this King Saul spirit, you'll be able to recognize some of these characteristics in people around you. The biggest problem that I'm currently seeing in the church is that this King Saul spirit has a lot of us caught up in the spear-throwing business. Go to church on Sunday and listen to how many Christians are gossiping, criticizing, and judging other Christians. They are busy hurting and fighting each other, instead of standing together in agreement and attacking the enemy. We're destroying each other and our churches instead of the enemy. This is not worth it. No wonder we have so many problems in our churches. Let's stop this spirit, and let's reverse the affects of it, as well.

We're almost done with the characteristics of the King Saul spirit. There's a few left, but these are the most dangerous ones. Take a look at the next characteristic of the King Saul spirit.

CHAPTER 12

The Serious Change
in King Saul

DESPERATE AND
DISGUISED

—◊◊◊—

King Saul eventually stopped seeking to kill David, after David twice could have killed him, but showed mercy instead. So King Saul admitted he was wrong and promised not to harm David again. I think he realized that he was not going to be able to kill David.

> Then Saul said, "I have sinned. Return, my son David. <u>For I will harm you no more,</u> because my life was precious in your eyes this day. Indeed I have played the fool and erred exceedingly." Then Saul said to David, "May you be blessed, my son David! You shall both do great things and also still prevail."

So David went on his way, and Saul returned to his place.

    —1 Samuel 26:21, (emphasis mine)

David actually did not believe what King Saul had said, and thought that someday he would still die at the hand of King Saul. So David decided to flee to the Philistines and hide there, where he was relatively safe.

Now it happened that the Philistines gathered their armies together and decided to make war with Israel again. When Saul heard this, he called up his army and encamped at Gilboa, where they were to fight the Philistines. Because Samuel had died, King Saul had no one to turn to for help. King Saul saw the armies of the Philistines and became afraid again. It's funny that this first characteristic of the King Saul spirit, **fear,** showed up once again. So what could King Saul do? The only thing he knew to do was to go to God. We all know that's the correct thing to do, right? But God did not answer King Saul: not by dreams, or by the prophets, or even by speaking directly to him. Why? Well, remember that the Holy Spirit had departed from King Saul, which meant no more help from God.

When Saul saw the army of the Philistines, he was afraid, and his heart trembled greatly. And when Saul inquired of the Lord, the Lord did not answer him, either by dreams or by Urim or by the prophets.

    —1 Samuel 28:5-6, (emphasis mine)

The next thing King Saul had to do was find someone else to help him. The problem was he went looking for help in the wrong place. The same goes for us. If we aren't looking for help from God, the devil may offer his own assistance. King Saul went looking for help from a medium. He did not want anyone to recognize him, nor did he want the medium woman to recognize him, so he disguised himself. All he wanted was to know what to do with the Philistine attack.

> Then Saul said to his servants, "<u>Find me a woman who is a medium,</u> that I may go to her and inquire of her." And his servants said to him, "In fact, there is a woman who is a medium at En Dor." <u>So Saul disguised himself</u> and <u>put on other clothes,</u> and he went, and two men with him; and they came to the woman by night. And he said, "Please conduct a seance for me, and bring up for me the one I shall name to you."
> — 1 Samuel 28:7-8, (emphasis mine)

Well, King Saul was the one who had removed and banned all the mediums and witches from the land. Now he was asking one to help him. You see, this act of King Saul was as foolish as his first foolish act, when he took the place of Samuel and offered a burnt offering to God in Gilgal. God had never told him to do it and also never told him to seek a medium. Now we must remember that King Saul was back-slidden and was not serving God, although he asked

God for help. King Saul's relationship with God was not right, so God could not help him. The Holy Spirit had departed from King Saul, and he had no more help. This chosen, anointed man of God, who had a changed heart, had sunk so low that he had to go seek help from a medium. King Saul must have known this was the wrong thing to do. Nevertheless, when you're desperate for help and you don't have the Holy Spirit with you, you'll most probably run to the world for help. That's exactly what King Saul did. Now remember, God told His people to stay away from these mediums.

> Give no regard to mediums and familiar spirits; do not seek after them, to be defiled by them: I am the Lord your God.
> —Leviticus 19:31, (emphasis mine)

> And the person who turns to mediums and familiar spirits, to prostitute himself with them, I will set My face against that person and cut him off from his people. Consecrate yourselves therefore, and be holy, for I am the Lord your God.
> —Leviticus 20:6-7, (emphasis mine)

God made it clear that the Israelites should not get entangled with mediums, familiar spirits, or witchcraft. Well, if you're in rebellion toward God's Word, what do you expect? The person's going to do what he needs to do. He won't listen to God's Word. That's what King Saul did; he listened to the King

Saul spirit and sought the medium. This anointed man of God had to go to the world for help. He had to disguise himself, as well, to get an answer from the medium woman. King Saul asked her to call up Samuel's spirit. This again was against God's law. He never wanted the Israelites to call up dead spirits. King Saul knew the law, but still went ahead and did it. The same old prideful, self-willed, disobedient attitude was still present in his life.

> There shall not be found among you anyone who makes his son or his daughter pass through the fire, or one who practices witch-craft, or a soothsayer, or one who interprets omens, or a sorcerer, or one who conjures spells, or a medium, or a spiritist, or <u>one who calls up the dead.</u> For all who do these things are an abomination to the Lord, and because of these abominations the Lord your God drives them out from before you.
> —Deuteronomy 18:10-12, (emphasis mine)

God didn't want them to mix with people who called up the dead. It just shows you how backslidden King Saul was. He knew these laws, but he was still disobedient to God's Word. So they continued and supposedly called up Samuel. I personally do not believe that God would allow Samuel to be called up from the dead to speak to King Saul. I believe that it was a familiar spirit, who was familiar with the circumstances, knew what had happened, and was imitating Samuel. There is no proof that it was

Samuel. King Saul only perceived it was Samuel, he did not see him (**v 14**). If God did not want to answer King Saul personally, why would He allow Samuel's spirit to be called up from the dead to answer him? God is against such practices. He wouldn't go against His own Word.

> So he said to her, "What is his form?" And she said, "An old man is coming up, and he is covered with a mantle." And Saul <u>perceived</u> that it was Samuel, and he stooped with his face to the ground and bowed down.
> — 1 Samuel 28:14, (emphasis mine)

> And when they say to you, "Seek those who are mediums and wizards, who whisper and mutter," <u>should not a people seek their God? Should they seek the dead on behalf of the living?</u>
> — Isaiah 8:19, (emphasis mine)

God would not allow this method to call up His prophet's spirit. This was a demonic practice. The session ended when King Saul was told by this familiar spirit that Israel was going to be defeated and King Saul was going to die. Saul was told that both he and his son Jonathan were going to die.

The same thing can happen to Christians in church as well. After trying to kill the children of God, they realize they are in trouble. When the enemy (the devil) wants to attack them, they run to God. But because of their poor relationship with God and because of the attack of the King Saul spirit, they no longer hear from God. So these people become so desperate for help that they run to the world. They've messed up and lied so much that they don't realize all they have to do is repent and confess. God always will forgive them and take them back. This King Saul spirit has so deceived them that they don't believe they can be accepted, or forgiven by God again. So they run to the world for help. They start going to nightclubs. They seek help from their drinking buddies and start using drugs, doing anything they can, just to be accepted again. Some will go to fortune tellers. Some will get involved in witchcraft or Wicca. Some even get involved with Satanism. They think the world can help them. They don't want the people to recognize them as a Christian, who used to testify about the love of God, so they disguise themselves. They don't admit that they used to be a Christian. They seek help from the world, but the problem is the world can't help them.

Summary of this chapter: My dear friend, I have been telling you throughout this whole book of how destructive this King Saul spirit can be. I've shown you how it leads people from fear, to impatience, to self-will, to disobedience, pride, and foolishness. You've seen how distressing and troublesome it can be to other people . . . how this spirit makes people lie, how they falsely accuse their friends, become rebellious, and how the Holy Spirit departs from them. You've seen how they get so jealous that they want to throw spears at and kill their fellow Christians. They can even split up churches. Then this King Saul spirit sends them to the world, where they have to disguise themselves. They can't be recognized as the Christian who used to witness about Jesus. What are these poor Christians going to do? Well, I have bad news. Everything you've heard and read so far is not really the main aim of this King Saul spirit. Yes, the King Saul spirit wants to destroy God's church and believers. It wants to use the anointed Christian to do the dirty work and destroy their anointed brothers and sisters, as we've read.

Apart from all the destructive work that the King Saul spirit already has done, its main aim is to kill the person it's using and attacking. You and I can be used by the King Saul spirit to kill other Christians and split up churches, but it really wants us to kill ourselves.

This is the last and final characteristic of the King Saul spirit: committing spiritual suicide.

CHAPTER 13

The Serious Change
in King Saul

COMMITTING SUICIDE

—⁓—

At last, we know the real motive of this demonic King Saul spirit. When I was making a study about this King Saul spirit, everything made sense to me, except I could not get behind the real motive of it. I knew there was something deeper causing Christians to hurt one another and backslide, or split up churches. Now, doing such things is evil. That's why I've spent so much time explaining to you what this demonic spirit does. So I knew there had to be a hidden agenda. What is this hidden agenda?

After we've destroyed the lives of our fellow Christians and split up the church, the King Saul spirit wants us to **commit spiritual suicide**. It wants you and me dead. What an evil, deceiving, demonic spirit! Let's go to the last chapter in 1 Samuel.

Now the Philistines fought against Israel; and the men of Israel fled from before the Philistines, and fell slain on Mount Gilboa. Then the Philistines followed hard after Saul and his sons. And the Philistines <u>killed Jonathan, Abinadab, and Malchishua, Saul's sons.</u> The battle became fierce against Saul. The archers hit him, and he was severely wounded by the archers. Then Saul said to his armorbearer, "Draw your sword, and thrust me through with it, lest these uncircumcised men come and thrust me through and abuse me." But his armorbearer would not, for he was greatly afraid. <u>Therefore Saul took a sword and fell on it.</u> And when his armorbearer saw that Saul was dead, <u>he also fell on his sword, and died with him.</u> So Saul, his three sons, his armorbearer, <u>and all his men died together that same day.</u>

— 1 Samuel 31:1-6, (emphasis mine)

There you have it. The fight had begun, and the Philistines were killing the Israelites. They killed Jonathan and all of King Saul's sons. Then they wounded King Saul. King Saul was not going to allow the enemy to kill him, so he asked his armor bearer to do it. The armor bearer was too afraid to kill his king. So what happened? King Saul **committed suicide**. He fell on a sword and killed himself. Unfortunately, the armor bearer, when he saw what the king had done, did the same thing; he also killed himself.

You see, it rubs off onto other people. That day King Saul, his sons, and all the men died. The King Saul spirit *eventually* had achieved its goal. It killed the chosen man of God himself, through **suicide**.

My dear brothers and sisters, this King Saul spirit does not only want you and me to kill one another, it wants us to kill ourselves, too. The King Saul spirit is basically a suicide spirit.

The Christian who has been attacked and used by this King Saul spirit, even after disguising himself and going to the world for help, eventually will realize that there is no hope against the enemy. Unfortunately they get sucked up into the world, and before you know it, they're altogether out of church, totally denying God, lost, and on their way to hell. I know this sounds harsh, but I've got to warn the church about this King Saul spirit. It's causing too much havoc in the lives of Christians. No wonder we're hearing of so many born-again Christians leaving the church, backsliding, and getting involved in Satanism, witchcraft, and many other false religions. They get to the point that their Christian lives are over, gone; they've committed spiritual suicide. They think it's too late to turn around, and most of them don't know what else to do except to go back into the world.

At this point, you may want to think of some other people you know who have gone through this attack. You can most probably figure out now why some of our fellow Christians are no longer in church or serving God. They want nothing to do with God. Well, they've committed spiritual suicide. They become hopeless, and there's nothing left for them to hold on to. Some people commit spiritual suicide, yes; but, unfortunately, some people also commit physical suicide and really die.

King Saul was chosen, anointed of God, had the Spirit of God, with God all the time, had been turned into another man, and was prophesying with a new heart. This man of God had been humble, peaceful, and helpful, but the King Saul spirit changed him into a murdering, destroying, self-destructing, suicidal person. What a way to go!

If you really get hold of this, you might realize that your own life has been affected by this spirit of suicide. Well, when I looked at my own life, I can see how I've killed many good things that came my way because I let this King Saul spirit control and use me. My friends, whoever allows this King Saul spirit to attack and control them eventually may end up committing spiritual suicide and losing their salvation. This means eternal damnation. This means hell, forever. It's not worth it, so we better change and stop this King Saul spirit. We can't afford to get to the point where we're killing and destroying ourselves, never mind our brothers and sisters and our churches.

What about Rob? What happened in that situation? Well, let's look at it. The last time we checked in, Rob was on the destruction path. He had become so jealous of the new singer, Thomas, that he was busy spearing him to the wall. Rob was doing everything possible to discredit Thomas. He used every trick in the book to badmouth Thomas and destroy him. Rob dug up some past issues in Thomas's life. He made life so miserable for him, with the help of some of the other Christians, of course, that poor Thomas had to fight and defend himself everywhere. Rob criticized Thomas about everything: his voice, his ways, everything he said or did . . . nothing was good enough. So Thomas tried staying out of Rob's way. Now remember that Thomas could have retaliated and attacked Rob as well. He could have brought up some of Rob's bad behavior, too, but he did not. He did not want to hurt another anointed man of God. Rob just steamrollered forward, using everyone and every situation to destroy Thomas spiritually. Thank heavens God was with Thomas, and Rob could never push Thomas to the breaking point or drag him into sin. Thomas just held on to what God had promised him. Many other people in the church started siding with Thomas, but many sided with Rob as well. Obviously the church split was on its way, but nobody could see it coming.

Well, Rob eventually saw that he was not going to get rid of Thomas, so he decided to get help from another source. Rob decided to stay in the church, but to go back into the world at the same time. He was so frustrated with himself and the situation that the King Saul spirit drove him further away from God, right into the arms of the world. Rob started drinking and smoking and doing worldly things, living a worldly life, but still coming to church. Most people knew who he was, but he would disguise himself when going out at night. He would act as if he had never been a Christian at all. He acted like a worldly person.

He started singing in a bar every Friday and Saturday evening. Rob totally backslid. He started believing in some other kind of religion. The new girlfriend he met in the bar didn't really help him either, because she believed in a false religion as well. Rob was a different person. He was back in the world. He was trying to get help from the worldly people, instead of repenting and coming back to God. The King Saul spirit still was not finished with poor Rob.

The suicide spirit had attacked Rob. It was only a matter of time before Rob would commit spiritual suicide. Then one day, this chosen, anointed, Holy Ghost-filled man, left the church and denied God because of the changes caused in him by the King Saul spirit. He wanted nothing more to do with God. He was using drugs, getting drunk, living an immoral life, and serving the devil. He had committed spiritual suicide. It was finished. Over and above **killing himself spiritually,** he took some other church members with him. He had led some people in the church to trust and believe in him. Many of them left the church when Rob did, and many of them never went back. Others tried a different church, but were not happy. The original church split up. It lost half of its members. The pastor was so devastated that he wanted to resign. The impact of this King Saul spirit was enormous. To think that it all started with a little bit of fear that Rob had developed.

Nobody could understand how such a loving, anointed, chosen, born-again, child of God could turn around and become a monster. One person, Rob, was the cause of many fellow Christians leaving the church, backsliding, and even committing spiritual suicide, just like he did.

The King Saul spirit got hold of Rob and other Christians, people like you and me . . . people who were born-again believers, chosen and anointed by God, full of the Holy Spirit, walking with God, prophesying in the church, who had new hearts and had been changed. These people allowed the King Saul spirit to attack them with fear, impatience, pride, disobedience, and self-will. They acted foolishly and distressed and troubled the other believers in the church. Rebellion started, and they began lying and accusing others of doing wrong. That's when the Holy Spirit departed from them and they backslid. Other evil spirits attacked them as well, and they became jealous. This made them mad, and they decided to destroy God's children, the other anointed of God. They started getting desperate for help, so they disguised themselves and went back into the world. They became worldly again and eventually committed spiritual suicide. They never returned to God, and eternal damnation became their future. Hell became their future home. These precious saints of God were just another part of Satan's deceitful plan to steal God's children. They were deceived by a cunning spirit. Their lives were destroyed because of this King Saul spirit, and no one could help them, because no one realized how dangerous this spirit was. Most people never even knew there was such a demonic spirit attacking their churches. No one realized that fear could lead to a spiritual death. Most people don't realize how these characteristics of the

King Saul spirit when they work in sequence, can be so devastating.

You or I, we could be Rob, you know? Rob was just the guy in the example, a true story by the way. It could be the pastor or assistant pastor being attacked. It could be the worship leader or one of the worship team members. What about the board member, or the deacon, trying to run the church and get the preacher fired because they don't like his new ideas? Oh yes, it could attack them, too, you're right. It could be the Sunday school teacher or the intercessor praying for the church. It could attack the person mowing the grass or mopping the floor. It could be the normal churchgoing member, who you think would never throw spears and split up the church. It could be any one of us. Are we allowing this to happen in our churches? Let's be honest: are we? Well, if we are, and we're not trying to stop it, we'll just end up destroying our brothers and sisters and our church. Then, when we've destroyed everyone else in our path, we'll end up harming and eventually killing ourselves. We'll be accountable for the mess, and we might end up dying spiritually and going to hell. This has happened, and it can happen again, if we don't stop this King Saul spirit.

"Is this the end?" you may ask. *"What can we do to stop this King Saul spirit? How do we counterattack it, or are we doomed?"* Oh no, we can counterattack and overcome the King Saul spirit. The only reason we're not doing it already is that we've never known about it. All of us know what fear, impatience, disobedience, and pride are. We know what

jealousy, rebellion, and lying are. We know what spear throwing is, because we've all gossiped and slandered, criticized and judged, haven't we? We've all encountered these characteristics of the King Saul spirit before; we know that, right? We've just never seen them work in a sequence, and this spirit uses the sequence of these characteristics to destroy us in the end. We've been ignorant. Remember what the Word says?

> My people are <u>destroyed for lack of knowledge.</u>
> Because you have rejected knowledge,
> I also will reject you from being priest for Me;
> Because you have forgotten the law of your God,
> I also will forget your children.
> —Hosea 4:6, (emphasis mine)

Remember that the King Saul spirit can attack you with any of its characteristics. It doesn't have to start with fear. It might start by letting you throw spears of gossip and criticism. It could start with the assistant pastor becoming jealous of the senior pastor. Everyone can be attacked differently, but the end result will be the same: death, or spiritual suicide, and a lot of damage done to the church and fellow Christians.

So next time you identify fear in your life towards a situation. Next time you become jealous towards a fellow Christian, or you start throwing those spears of gossip and criticism at them. Next time you feel like you're better than your brother or sister, watch out for pride. The next time you get impatient with people or situations, you must realize that the King Saul spirit is starting to attack and use you. Counterattack immediately, or else, chaos will follow. Don't think it's just a little fear, anger, jealousy or just gossip, and that it will go away by itself. No, we have to identify these characteristics and resist them by the power of God.

Summary of Part One: What can I say about King Saul in closing? I want to emphasize one more time that Saul, who was chosen by God to be king, was anointed by God. God let the Holy Spirit come upon him. God promised to be with him, always. He started prophesying. He received a new heart from God and was changed into another man, just like the born-again child of God today. He had a purpose in life. God had called him for a specific task, to work for Him, to save His people. Unfortunately, he never reached that plan or goal in his life. He never achieved what God had called him to. He never lived out his purpose on earth. It was stolen from him by a demonic attack, which he allowed to take place. His whole life was turned into chaos, just because he gave in and allowed the King Saul spirit to use and attack him. He let fear, impatience, disobedience, and pride rule him. He became self-willed and acted foolishly. He troubled and distressed his people. He became rebellious and rejected God's Word. He lied and accused other people of the wrong things done. He lost his anointing, when the Holy Spirit departed from him, and then he became so jealous of another anointed man of God that he decided to kill him. He did everything in his power to murder David. He backslid and went into the world to look for help. King Saul eventually committed suicide. The effects of listening to and giving in to the characteristics of the King Saul spirit were devastating.

A promising king ended up being a disappointment, because of his smallness of character. He allowed the King Saul spirit characteristics to dominate his thought life and control him. The same thing will happen to you and me if we allow this spirit to control and use us.

What was the **cost** of allowing this King Saul spirit to enter his life?

1) It cost him the **Holy Spirit.** He lost the power of the anointing on his life (**1 Sam.16:14**).
2) God never spoke to him or listened to him again. He had no communication with God. Plainly, God stopped answering King Saul (**1 Sam. 28:6**).
3) God rejected him and chose someone else to do the job (**1 Sam. 16:1**).
4) He became a mass murderer (**1 Sam. 17–19**).
5) He backslid, went back into the world (**1 Sam. 28:7**).
6) He died in sin. He committed suicide (**1 Sam. 31:4**).

Don't let this happen to us or to our churches, my friend. Let's counterattack this King Saul spirit and get it removed from our lives.

PART TWO

COUNTERATTACKING THE KING SAUL SPIRIT

—⁓—

CHAPTER 1

The David Spirit

—⟋⟍—

So what's the first step in counterattacking the King Saul spirit? The first step is to identify this King Saul spirit in our own lives, and then to deal with it. Don't go looking for it in someone else. How do we identify it? Well, the first thing you have to do is to recognize that you're being attacked and used. If you don't think that this spirit is attacking you and using you, you'll do nothing about it and become ignorant toward it. Guess what? You can end up backsliding and committing spiritual suicide. You have to realize that you are a candidate for such an attack, at any time in your spiritual life. Once you've realized and recognized such an attack, then you can start to counterattack this King Saul spirit.

It's like getting sick. If you don't realize what virus or sickness you have, how are you going to treat it? You might think it's the flu, but when you get to the doctor, you find out it's actually a kidney infection. Now you can treat it and pray against it, because you've identified it. The same thing happens with the King Saul spirit. Maybe you've identified that you have **fear** or **pride**. You might recognize that you're a **gossiper and judgmental**. Maybe you're a **spear thrower**. Well, my friend, you've identified the attack in your life that's coming from the King Saul spirit. Now you can do something about it, right? We can overcome this King Saul spirit every time it shows up, and what a pleasure it will be to get it out of our churches. This is the difficult part, to admit that you're being attacked.

We're going to look at a man who was in the middle of this whole ordeal with King Saul. We will counterattack this King Saul spirit with a David spirit, or a David attitude. What is the David spirit or David attitude? To be able to answer this question, we will have to go and look at the life of David, to see what happened to him and how he handled his situation. David had counterattacked the King Saul spirit earlier. He was the only one who could get King Saul to calm down; the evil spirit left when David started playing and singing. David had something that we need, too. That's why we have to adapt a David attitude, or a David spirit. We can take David as an example, a man after God's own heart.

> And when He had removed him, He raised up for them David as king, to whom also He gave testimony and said, "I have found David the son of Jesse, <u>a man after My own heart,</u> who will do all My will."
> —Acts 13:22, (emphasis mine)

So let's see who David was and where he came from. This is going to be interesting, and I'm going to show you something that I had never seen before I started reading this story about King Saul and King David.

CHAPTER 2

Who Was David?

—⟆⟆—

D avid was the son of Jesse, from the tribe of Judah. Jesse had eight sons, and David was the youngest. His job was to tend the sheep in the fields. David, just like Saul, was minding his own business and just doing his job. One day, while he was playing his harp and singing about God, he was called home. He had to come quickly. There was a prophet, Samuel, who wanted to see him. Can you imagine how this young boy must have felt? He must have wondered what he could have done wrong that the prophet would want to see him. He had done nothing wrong. God had a calling on his life, but David did not know that. So he walked into the room, with all his brothers and father present, to meet with Samuel the prophet. David's life was about to change forever.

How did David end up being brought before the prophet Samuel? Well, God had **chosen** David to be the new king to replace King Saul. David was about to be **anointed** by God as the new king of Israel. What a change: from a shepherd boy to the king of Israel. It must have been a shock to poor David. Well, when David walked into the room, God said to Samuel, *"That's the one, **anoint** him king of Israel"* (**1 Sam. 6:12**). I think Samuel must have thought, *"Come on, God, look at this guy, he's so young and bright-eyed. Are you sure, Lord?"* God knew exactly what He was doing, and Samuel anointed David as the new king of Israel. David turned into King David. This time, it was not the people who asked for a king, but God who **chose** and **appointed** them a king. That was the difference between King Saul's appointment as king and King David's. This is how it happened.

> "Then invite Jesse to the sacrifice, and I will show you what you shall do; you shall anoint for Me the one I name to you." . . . So he sent and brought him in. Now he was ruddy, with bright eyes, and good-looking. And the LORD said, "<u>Arise, anoint him; for this is the one!</u>" Then Samuel took the horn of oil and anointed him in the midst of his brothers; <u>and the Spirit of the LORD came upon David</u> from that day forward. So Samuel arose and went to Ramah.
>
> —1 Samuel 16:3, 12-13, (emphasis mine)

If we look at this verse we realize that God showed Samuel the one He had chosen (**1 Sam. 16:3**), so David was **chosen** by God. God told Samuel to **anoint** David, so David was **anointed** by God through the prophet (**1 Sam. 16:12**). After

the anointing, the **Spirit of the Lord** came upon
David **(1 Sam. 16:13).** David had **received the Holy
Spirit**. This sounds so familiar to me. If I'm not
mistaken, Saul went through the same procedures.
He was chosen by God, just like David was. Saul was
anointed by God through the prophet Samuel, so was
David. The Spirit of the Lord came upon Saul and
also upon David. At this point, Saul, David, and you
and I, my fellow believer, have had the same things
happen to us.

If we compare the born-again child of God today
with Saul and David, we all three have the same
spiritual qualities, right? In the first few chapters,
I was trying to explain how normal people with
these characteristics are capable of being attacked
and used by the King Saul spirit. Well, David was a
normal guy, too, just like you and me. He was good-
looking: ruddy with bright eyes, a handsome man.
If I remember correctly Saul was a handsome man,
too, but taller than David. David, no doubt, had rosy
cheeks and auburn or golden hair. We see the similarities between Saul and David, but David had his
own unique qualities. Let's look at the facts and characteristics of King David.

Characteristics and facts about David:

1) David was **chosen** by God: *"Now the Lord
said to Samuel, 'How long will you mourn for
Saul, seeing I have rejected him from reigning
over Israel? Fill your horn with oil, and go; I
am sending you to Jesse the Bethlehemite. For*

I have <u>provided Myself a king</u> among his sons'"
(1 Sam. 16:1) (emphasis mine). God had <u>chosen</u>
David from Jesse's sons.

2) David was **anointed** by God: *"Then invite Jesse
to the sacrifice, and I will show you what you
shall do; <u>you shall anoint for Me </u>the one I name
to you"* **(1 Sam. 16:3)** (emphasis mine).

3) The **Spirit of the Lord** came upon David: *"Then
Samuel took the horn of oil and anointed him in
the midst of his brothers; and the <u>Spirit of the
Lord</u> <u>came upon David</u> from that day forward.
So Samuel arose and went to Ramah"* **(1 Sam.
16:13)** (emphasis mine).

4) **God was with** David **(1 Sam. 16:18)**.

5) David was a **skillful musician (1 Sam. 16:18)**.

6) David was **a mighty man of valor, a man of
war (1 Sam. 16:18)**.

7) David was **prudent in speech:** *"Then one of the
servants answered and said, 'Look, I have seen
a son of Jesse the Bethlehemite, who is <u>skillful
in playing, a mighty man of valor, a man of war,
prudent in speech,</u> and a handsome person; and
<u>the Lord is with him</u>'"* **(1 Sam. 16:18)** (emphasis
mine).

8) David had a **courageous** spirit. He had **no fear**
at all. Not like King Saul. David knew that **God
was with him** all the time. He was not afraid
of Goliath, the Philistine, like Saul was. He
did not sit around waiting for someone else to
go fight the enemy; no, David went out and
attacked the enemy and killed him. David let
King Saul know that he was not afraid of the

enemy *"'Your servant has killed both lion and bear; and this uncircumcised Philistine will be like one of them, seeing he has defied the armies of the living God.' Moreover David said, 'The Lord, who delivered me from the paw of the lion and from the paw of the bear, <u>He will deliver me from the hand of this Philistine</u>.' And Saul said to David, 'Go, and the Lord be with you!'"* **(1 Sam. 17:36-37)** (emphasis mine).

9) David had a **killing attitude** toward the enemy, not towards his fellow brothers, unlike King Saul. He killed the enemy, not his friends. *"Then David said to the Philistine, 'You come to me with a sword, with a spear, and with a javelin. But I come to you in the name of the Lord of hosts, the God of the armies of Israel, whom you have defied. This day <u>the Lord will deliver you into my hand,</u> and <u>I will strike you and take your head from you.</u> And this day I will give the carcasses of the camp of the Philistines to the birds of the air and the wild beasts of the earth, that all the earth may know that there is a God in Israel"* **(1 Sam. 17:45-46)** (emphasis mine). David was bold for God.

10) David had an **obedient spirit**. He would not touch, never mind kill, God's anointed. Two times he had the opportunity to kill King Saul, his rival, but he refused to go against the Word of God. You see, even if King Saul had backslidden and was hunting David, trying to kill him, David did not want to be **disobedient**. David feared God and respected His Word more

143

than man. The first time David had the opportunity to kill King Saul, this is what happened.

Then the men of David said to him, "This
is the day of which the Lord said to you,
'Behold, I will deliver your enemy into your
hand that you may do to him as it seems good
to you.'" And David arose and secretly cut
off a corner of Saul's robe. Now it happened
afterward that David's heart troubled him
because he had cut Saul's robe. And he said
to his men, 'The Lord forbid that I should do
this thing to my master, the <u>Lord's anointed,
to stretch out my hand against him, seeing
he is the anointed of the Lord.'</u> So David
restrained his servants with these words, and
did not allow them to rise against Saul. And
Saul got up from the cave and went on his
way.

— 1 Samuel 24:4-7, (emphasis mine)

David realized that King Saul was still the
anointed of God in God's eyes. We cannot decide
who's the anointed of God and who's not. That's
God's privilege. David remembered the Words of
the Lord, and he was not going to be disobedient to
them. He was so sensitive towards God's anointed
that he felt guilty for cutting off the corner of King
Saul's robe. You see, with this kind of attitude one
can withstand and even counterattack the King Saul
spirit. God specifically said we should not touch his
anointed children. That includes all believers.

Saying, "Do not touch My anointed ones, and
do My prophets no harm."
                    —Psalm 105:15, (emphasis mine)

The second time David could have killed King
Saul; he almost had the same experience.

Then David answered, and said to
Ahimelech the Hittite and to Abishai the son
of Zeruiah, brother of Joab, saying, "Who
will go down with me to Saul in the camp?"
And Abishai said, "I will go down with you."
So David and Abishai came to the people by
night; and there Saul lay sleeping within the
camp, with his spear stuck in the ground by
his head. And Abner and the people lay all
around him. Then Abishai said to David, "God
has delivered your enemy into your hand this
day. Now therefore, please, let me strike him
at once with the spear, right to the earth; and
I will not have to strike him a second time!"
And David said to Abishai, "Do not destroy
him; for who can stretch out his hand against
the Lord's anointed, and be guiltless?" David
said furthermore, "As the Lord lives, the Lord
shall strike him, or his day shall come to die,
or he shall go out to battle and perish.
The Lord forbid that I should stretch out
my hand against the Lord's anointed. But
please, take now the spear and the jug of
water that are by his head, and let us go."
                    —1 Samuel 26:6-11, (emphasis mine)

Now this was interesting. When David and his companion were inside the camp, Abishai, who was with him, asked David if he could spear King Saul and kill him. What a great answer David gave this young man. David did not allow this King Saul spirit to control him; no, he told Abishai that you don't spear the anointed of God. Does it sound familiar? The King Saul spirit would have speared the person. David knew that to spear your anointed brother was to go against God's Word. At the same time you don't allow others to spear God's anointed, you stop them if you can.

It doesn't matter if you have the best opportunity to throw spears of gossip or criticism or judgment toward your anointed brother or sister. You don't have to kill them and pin them to the wall with your spears. Even if they're in the wrong, they're still God's anointed. David knew that if he had done so, then he would have been just as guilty and evil as King Saul. David realized you cannot stretch out your hand toward God's anointed and remain guiltless. If only modern-day Christians would get hold of this principle. There are too many anointed men and women stretching out their hands toward other anointed men and women of God, killing them spiritually. Let me give you some important news. People who spear their fellow brothers and sisters won't be guiltless before God. David realized he should leave King Saul to God. God would make sure that King Saul would receive his fair punishment. If anyone was going to kill King Saul, it would have had to be because God allowed it. He could die in battle, but not by the hand of David. We can learn from David's attitude. We should adapt this kind of thinking, so that we can counterattack and neutralize this King Saul spirit. Now remember, David was **anointed by God** to be the next king. However, King Saul still was the king, so it would have been easy for David to have given in to the same King Saul spirit that had attacked King Saul. David would have been king if Saul was dead, but he still did not pay heed to the King Saul spirit and kill King Saul.

By now we know that King Saul eventually would commit suicide, making David the king of Israel.

> Therefore all the elders of Israel came to the king at Hebron, and King David made a covenant with them at Hebron before the Lord. And they <u>anointed David king over Israel.</u>
> —2 Samuel 5:3, (emphasis mine)

King David reigned for forty years as the king of Israel. He won many battles and achieved great things for the Lord, the Lord being with him always. David was the kind of king that any nation would want. He was powerful, rich, strong, a mighty man of war, and most of all a true man of God. He was an obedient man and always inquired from God what he should do. He had a good relationship with God. What a blessing! He represented the born-again believer in today's life. Oh, yes, he made mistakes, like everyone else, but nothing like the evil King Saul, who backslid and yielded to the King Saul spirit. David was different; he was full of the Holy Spirit and everyone loved him. He was man after God's own heart.

So David was withstanding and neutralizing this King Saul spirit, right? He was doing good, counteracting it. David was doing everything God had told him to do. What I'm going to tell you now may shock you. There came a day when David was not watching out for this King Saul spirit. He was too at ease and too assured of himself. Before he knew it, the King Saul spirit had attacked him, too. Some may be asking, *"Why on earth would the King Saul spirit want to attack King David?"* The reason is simple. It wanted to destroy David, too. David wasn't any different than any of us, or King Saul, do you remember? David had all the characteristics that Saul had and we have: chosen by God, anointed by God, full of the Holy Spirit, accompanied by God. David was going to be used by God, so he was a good candidate to be attacked by the King Saul spirit too, just as King Saul was attacked by it.

Summary of this chapter: Let's put it this way: why would the King Saul spirit _not_ attack King David? Let me tell you something: this King Saul spirit would have destroyed King David a long time ago, if it could have done so. The only reason it hadn't was because King David was obedient to God's Word and feared God with a passion. David gave the King Saul spirit no open door. Nevertheless, the day came when the King Saul spirit saw the opportunity; it stepped right in and began the destruction. Before David knew what had hit him, he was in trouble. The King Saul spirit had struck again.

CHAPTER 3

The Change in King David

—⟳—

Well, what happened? How did this King Saul spirit attack King David? How did it enter in to David's life? David was not attacked with fear, or impatience, or even pride. David was attacked when he was in the wrong place at the wrong time. The king should have been making war with the enemy, because it was the time of year to make war. David was not where he should have been. He was **disobedient** to what he was supposed to be doing. All kings were out fighting. David had decided he was not going to war and sent Joab to be in charge. Maybe David was tired and just didn't feel like going. Maybe he was just lazy. Maybe he was deceived by the devil, telling him not to go, that he needn't go. We can't know for sure. The fact is that he hadn't followed the usual routine of the kings. He should not have been home.

> It happened in the spring of the year, at the time when kings go out to battle, that David sent Joab and his servants with him, and all Israel; and they destroyed the people of Ammon and besieged Rabbah. <u>But David remained at Jerusalem.</u>
>
> —2 Samuel 11:1, (emphasis mine)

Now we all know that **disobedience** is one of the characteristics of the King Saul spirit. This is where the King Saul spirit started to attack King David, through **disobedience**. Let's see what happened. Just remember that it was David who opened the door to the King Saul spirit. If he had not been disobedient, this spirit could not have attacked and controlled him. That's why it's so important for you and me to recognize the characteristics of the King Saul spirit when they show up. As soon as we recognize that they're attacking or using us, we should counterattack. The moment you and I experience fear, impatience, pride, disobedience, jealousy, or even deceitfulness in our lives, we should immediately recognize the attack from the King Saul spirit and start counterattacking. Whenever we recognize any of the King Saul spirit characteristics, we should retaliate and stop this destructive demon spirit in its tracks. We have the power to do that, my friend. God gave us the Word of God, the name of Jesus, and the blood of Jesus. God gave us His angels to surround and protect us, so that no evil or King Saul spirit can harm us. We have the power of the Holy Spirit in us. We have the armor of God to protect us. We have the fruit of the Spirit available to us, and remember that one of the fruits is "self control" **(Gal. 5:22)**. So we have all the means; we can counterattack this King Saul spirit. God has given us the weapons to do so.

David should have recognized the problem and made it right, but he didn't. This allowed the King Saul spirit to start its destructive path. It attacked King David and actually started using him, the man after God's own heart. Who would have thought that David would be trapped by the King Saul spirit? The man had been so in tune with God that he would not kill King Saul, the anointed of God. Yet, he got attacked and used by the King Saul spirit. Can you see that even if you're doing well in your Christian walk with God, there is always the possibility of being attacked by this demon spirit? So be careful what you do, how you act, and always be on the lookout for this deceiving King Saul spirit. Ask God for discernment.

David became disobedient. He stayed at home instead of going to war. David would not have been tempted by sin if he had gone with the army, and he would not have been attacked by the King Saul spirit in this particular way.

So one night, as the tradition was in those days, David was walking on the roof of his house enjoying the cool night breeze. Like most houses then, the roof was flat, and people slept there in the summer to be cooler. Here's a bit of background: the Hebrews, like other Orientals, rose at daybreak and always took a nap during the heat of the day. Afterward, they lounged in the cool of the evening on their flat-roofed terraces. It is probable that David had ascended to enjoy the open-air refreshment earlier than usual. Then, while he was walking, he noticed a woman bathing. She was very beautiful, and the king liked what he saw.

> Then it happened one evening that David arose from his bed and walked on the roof of the king's house. And from the roof he <u>saw a woman bathing,</u> and <u>the woman was very beautiful</u> to behold.
> —2 Samuel 11:2, (emphasis mine)

David was attacked by a spirit of **lust or greed**. He wanted this woman. So the king made inquiries to find out who she was. The word got back quickly that her name was Bathsheba. The problem was that she was married. This is where King David should have said, *"Okay, I will move on and forget this woman, because the Word says not to commit adultery."* King David knew the Word and should have obeyed it. But this was different: it was a beautiful woman, and the King Saul spirit had found the gap through King David's disobedience. So, David became **rebellious** and rejected what the Word of God had said about this issue. This could cost him his life, but he was prepared to take the gamble. Come on, King David knew better than that. Well, he was being controlled by the King Saul spirit, even if it meant death.

> The man who commits <u>adultery</u> with another man's wife, he who commits adultery with

his neighbor's wife, <u>the adulterer and the adulteress, shall surely be put to death.</u>
    —Leviticus 20:10, (emphasis mine)

King David went ahead and let the woman come to him. Then he committed adultery with her. How sad. They both knew the punishment for adultery, but still went ahead and took the chance. He had become **jealous** of Uriah the Hittite, who was married to Bathsheba. In those days, when a king or ruler was interested in a woman, he would send an officer to her home to take her to the palace. She was assigned an apartment, and if she was chosen to be his wife, an announcement was made accordingly. In David's case, the woman already was married, and David could not have gone through the normal ritual. She could not be put up in an apartment; she was already married. So this was pure lust and adultery. Bathsheba got pregnant, of course, and now there was trouble. They had to do something, but what?

So David sent and inquired about the woman. And someone said, "Is this not <u>Bathsheba, the daughter of Eliam, <u>the wife of Uriah</u> the Hittite?" Then David sent messengers, and took her; and she came to him, and <u>he lay with her,</u> for she was cleansed from her impurity; and she returned to her house. And the woman <u>conceived;</u> so she sent and told David, and said, "<u>I am with child.</u>"
    —2 Samuel 11:3-4, (emphasis mine)

Some immediate measures of hiding their sin were necessary, for the king's honor as well as Bathsheba's safety, since an adulterous act was punished with death. **Leviticus 20:10** says, *"The man who commits adultery with another man's wife, he who commits adultery with his neighbor's wife, the adulterer and the adulteress, shall surely be put to death"* (emphasis mine).

This is where the King Saul spirit brought in the **fear.** David and Bathsheba must have been afraid that people would find out and they would be put to death. So David had a plan. Unfortunately, it was the plan of the King Saul spirit, because that's who was in control of David's life at that point of time. He was going to **deceive** Uriah and the people. The **lying** spirit had showed up. David was not going to take the blame for the mess he was in, so he formulated a plan to "blame" Uriah for the pregnancy. Do you recognize some of the King Saul spirit characteristics: disobedience, fear, lying (deceit) and jealousy?

So David had Uriah brought home from the battlefield. He spoke to Uriah to find out what was going on with the war and how everyone was doing. Then he urged him to go home to his wife and spend some time with her. He was hoping that Uriah would sleep with Bathsheba. That would solve the problem, because then David's child could be seen as Uriah's child, and no one would know that King David and Bathsheba had committed adultery. You see, King David was trying to cover up his sin. The bad news is that the Scripture says differently. If you sin against the Lord, your sin will find you out.

But if you do not do so, then take note, you have sinned against the Lord; and be sure <u>your sin will find you out.</u>
> —Numbers 32:23, (emphasis mine)

What King David had asked Uriah to do, he did not do; he went and slept at the door of the king's house with the other servants. Uriah was a faithful man and very considerate toward his fellow soldiers. So King David's plan did not work.

And David said to Uriah, "<u>Go down to your house and wash your feet.</u>" So Uriah departed from the king's house, and a gift of food from the king followed him.
But <u>Uriah slept at the door of the king's house with all the servants of his lord, and did not go down to his house.</u>
> —2 Samuel 11:8-9, (emphasis mine)

Uriah chose not to be spoilt while his fellow soldiers were fighting and sleeping in tents and in the field. He just wouldn't allow himself to have these privileges not allowed his friends, who were still at war. So King David had to make another plan. He called Uriah and invited him to sit down and eat with him. Wow, what a privilege to eat with the king! Then he made Uriah drunk, hoping to get him to his wife Bathsheba, to sleep with her. The plan, unfortunately, did not work either. Uriah refused to go to his wife. David became desperate.

Now when David called him, he ate and drank before him; <u>and he made him drunk.</u> And at evening he went out to lie on his bed with the servants of his lord, <u>but he did not go down to his house.</u>
                              —2 Samuel 11:13, (emphasis mine)

Making a man drunk is a sin in itself; so instead of solving his problem, David became more deeply involved in sin. So what could David do? He could have spoken the truth, you know, but he chose to listen to the King Saul spirit. What happened next is the same thing that happened to King Saul a few years earlier. The murdering spirit came upon King David, the same spirit that came upon King Saul. David had been attacked by the same destructive King Saul spirit. David was planning to have Uriah killed in combat. He wrote a letter with certain instructions in it, and gave it to Uriah to give to Joab. The instructions were clear and preplanned: *"Put Uriah in the front row of the hottest battle, get away from him, so that he could be killed by the enemy"* (**2 Sam. 11:14-15**). David had set Uriah up to be murdered. King David was doing exactly what King Saul had done to him, all because he allowed the King Saul spirit to dictate and control his life.

Uriah carried the letter concerning himself back to Joab, never realizing that his king would stoop so low in sin. The letter contained Uriah's own death sentence. In his desperation, David thought his only escape was the death of Uriah. He had the power to make it appear legal, but God called this sin by its proper name—"murder"—and laid the charge to David.

> In the morning it happened that David wrote a letter to Joab and sent it by the hand of Uriah. And he wrote in the letter, saying, "<u>Set Uriah in the forefront of the hottest battle, and retreat from him, that he may be struck down and die.</u>"
> —2 Samuel 11:14-15, (emphasis mine)

King David now had stooped as low and become as wicked as King Saul. I believe that David was not hearing from God; that's for sure. The Holy Spirit is our helper, right? Don't tell me the Holy Spirit did not try and warn King David when he looked upon Bathsheba bathing. Don't tell me the Holy Spirit didn't try and stop King David from sleeping with her, deceiving, and then killing Uriah. The Holy Spirit will always tell you, *"No, don't do that; it's wrong, it's sin."* No child of God, who is truly serving God and walking in the Spirit, should do such a thing. David did not kill King Saul earlier on, so why did he have Uriah killed? Well, with King Saul's episode, David did not allow the King Saul spirit to control him. With Uriah's episode, David invited this King Saul spirit right into his life, and it started to control and use him.

The battle started and ended just as King David intended. Many soldiers were killed that day, but the most important one was Uriah. With Uriah dead, Bathsheba and David were free to continue their association and cover their initial sin. How low could a man of God go, to sin to the point of being glad when one of his servants and friends was dead! Yet, this was David's first reaction: relief from the fear of exposure of his sin. He thought all would be well now, but he failed to reckon with God, the Judge of all, who demands justice from His servants. David knew better, but still listened to the King Saul spirit instead of listening to God's Word. The **disobedience** turned into greed and **jealousy** for another man's wife. **Sin** took place. This brought **fear**, which led to **lying**. The **killing spirit** showed up, and King David (the chosen, anointed man of God, full of the Holy Spirit, accompanied by God) was attacked and used by the King Saul spirit to destroy a marriage and kill a man.

> Then the men of the city came out and fought with Joab. And some of the people of the servants of David fell; and Uriah the Hittite died also.
> —2 Samuel 11:17, (emphasis mine)

The messenger brought the word that Uriah was dead. The King Saul spirit had achieved its goal: the killing of a saint of God by another saint of God. People were very sad, obviously, and so was Bathsheba. She mourned for her husband. Funny thing is, though she mourned her husband, Bathsheba was willing to eventually marry the very man who had caused his death. The mourning lasted about seven days, and right after it, Bathsheba was back with King David. They had a hurried marriage, to hide her pregnancy and fool the people, but it could not be hidden from God. David's actions displeased God. All sin displeases God, who will in due time render to all men justice, according to their works.

> When the wife of Uriah heard that Uriah her husband was dead, <u>she mourned for her husband.</u> And when <u>her mourning was over,</u> David sent and brought her to his house, and she <u>became his wife and bore him a son.</u> But <u>the thing that David had done displeased the Lord.</u>
> —2 Samuel 11:26-27, (emphasis mine)

Don't forget, the main aim of the King Saul spirit is to kill the person it has attacked. It still wanted King David to commit suicide, too, just like King Saul. So the King Saul spirit had not finished its work yet. It still had to destroy King David. Let's see if it could achieve that goal.

I hope you're still with me. I'm trying to show you how any man after God's heart can make a mistake and let the King Saul spirit attack and use him. If he allows this spirit to use him, it can harm, destroy, and even kill his friends, his fellow brothers and sisters in the Lord, just like it did with David.

I'm sure King David and his new wife Bathsheba thought that everything was going to be alright. All the evidence had been neutralized. Bathsheba was almost due with the baby, and dad David was doing well. His armies had won many battles, and the land was in good shape. The people were deceived by King David and his wife, but God was not. So God sent the prophet, Nathan, to King David. Nathan told King David of a problem between two people and asked if the king could give a punishment to the guilty party. The story angered King David, and he ruled that the guilty man should die, restoring back to the other man fourfold. It was a harsh punishment to give. If only King David knew that he had spoken his own punishment over himself.

> So David's anger was greatly aroused against the man, and he said to Nathan, "As the Lord lives, the man who has done this shall surely die! And he shall restore fourfold for the lamb, because he did this thing and because he had no pity."
>
> —2 Samuel 12:5-6

Nathan accepted the rule of the king and then spoke the final Words from God. He told King David that he, the king, was this guilty man. Nathan also told King David that God knew about the sin that David had committed, even if the people did not know. He explained in detail what the consequences were going to be in King David's and his family's lives. Remember that the wages of sin is death.

> For the wages of sin is death, but the gift of God is eternal life in Christ Jesus our Lord.
>
> —Romans 6:23

God told David that He was going to expose this sin to the whole of Israel. There were going to be consequences for the sin he had committed.

> Then Nathan said to David, "You are the man! Thus says the Lord God of Israel: 'I anointed you king over Israel, and I delivered you from the hand of Saul. . . . Why have you despised the commandment of the LORD, to do evil in His sight? You have killed Uriah the Hittite with the sword; you have taken his wife to be your wife, and have killed him with the sword of the people of Ammon. . . . For you did it secretly, but I will do this thing before all Israel, before the sun.'"
>   —2 Samuel 12:7, 9, 12, (emphasis mine)

I have told you to adapt the King David attitude and the King David Spirit, which can counterattack the King Saul spirit. How does this work? King David now was used and controlled by this very spirit!

Well, I was talking about the David we learned about earlier on in this chapter: the David who would not give in to fear, impatience, disobedience, and pride, who was not self-willed rebellious, jealous, or deceitful. The David who would not kill King Saul because the Word of God said not to touch God's anointed. I'm talking about the David who killed the enemy, Goliath, not his fellow brothers and sisters. That handsome, courageous man of war, the man who was also a gentle man, a singer, playing music that made the demon spirits flee; that's the David I'm talking about. So, yes, we have to adapt the David attitude and David spirit toward our fellow brothers and sisters in Christ. My job is to show you how easy it is for any person to be attacked and be used by the King Saul spirit. Let's face it, if a man like King David can be deceived and attacked by the King Saul spirit, so can we.

Summary of this chapter: David's downfall is especially discouraging after he'd been such an example to all of us. Yes, it's sad, but it also teaches us a lesson. *Nobody* is immune to this King Saul spirit: even men that are men after God's own heart can fall, even us. God knows about every scheme that wicked people are planning. He knows about the board who's trying to get rid of the pastor. He knows about the pastor trying to control the church members and the finances. He knows about every spear of gossip, criticism, unforgiveness and hate that Christians have thrown towards each other. God knows about the destruction that man wants to do to His church and His people. God knows everything, while man thinks that no one will find out their plans and sins. Well, God knows about them all and we'll have to give account of every one of those evil wicked deeds we've done to each other.

It just makes us realize that when it happens to us, we shouldn't feel condemned, but rather convicted. The sooner we realize we're wrong, the sooner we can repent, confess, and make right with God and with the people involved. The Holy Spirit will help us; I know that for sure, because He's our Helper.

So what did King David do to get out the mess he was in?

CHAPTER 4

David's Counterattack

—⟋⟋⟋—

The King Saul spirit was still planning to get King David to surrender completely. It wanted David to say, *"That's it; I'm finished. The people know, God knows. I've displeased God; I've killed a man; I'm a sinner; I've broken the trust of the people; and I'm a failure. I'm no better than King Saul. I might as well end it all."*

If King David had done that, he would have played right into the hand of the King Saul spirit and committed spiritual suicide. Thank heavens he didn't do it. King David counterattacked the King Saul spirit. How? Well, like King Saul, he admitted that he was wrong and that he had sinned, but with a difference. David did not ask Nathan the prophet to forgive him, but confessed and repented to God. I need you to see the difference. King Saul also admitted that he had sinned, but asked Samuel to forgive him, **(1 Samuel 15:24, 26).** What about God? King David was different. He repented and then stopped the willful sin. He never committed the same sins of adultery and murder again. That was true repentance. King Saul, on the contrary, did not show true repentance. He confessed and repented, but did not mean it. Why? Well, after repenting, he did not turn away from the sin, but committed it again. That's called false repentance! Let's look at the different incidents.

Saul's repentance:

When King Saul first opened himself up to the King Saul spirit at Gilgal (becoming fearful, impatient, self-willed, prideful, and disobedient), remember that he did not repent or admit his wrong at all (**1 Sam. 13:8-15**).

The second time he fell into sin, he was supposed to destroy all of the Amelekites. He did not do so, but spared Agag the King and kept back all of the best animals, supposedly for a sacrifice to God (**1 Sam. 15:3-23**). At least King Saul repented and confessed this time, but he continued his disobedience toward God's Word.

> Then Saul said to Samuel, "I have sinned, for I have transgressed the commandment of the Lord and your words, because I feared the people and obeyed their voice. Now therefore, please pardon my sin, and return with me, that I may worship the Lord." Then he said, "I have sinned; yet honor me now, please, before the elders of my people and

before Israel, and return with me, that I may worship the LORD your God."
— 1 Samuel 15:24-25, (emphasis mine)

It looks like all that King Saul was worried about was himself. He asked Samuel to forgive or pardon him, so that he could go worship the Lord. Still he continued in his willful sin, until the Holy Spirit departed from him and an evil spirit attacked him. Saul's repentance was never real. How many times did he promise not to seek David or attempt to kill him? He even promised Jonathan, his son, that he would stop trying to kill David. *"So Saul heeded the voice of Jonathan, and Saul swore, 'As the LORD lives, <u>he shall not be killed'"</u>* **(1 Sam. 19:6)** (emphasis mine). Every time, he just went right back and heeded to the King Saul spirit and tried to have David killed again.

King Saul never truly repented from any of the willful sins he committed. That's why the Holy Spirit eventually departed from him. I'm sure the Holy Spirit also tried to warn King Saul not to be disobedient, jealous, prideful, and impatient. The Holy Spirit must have told King Saul not to spare Agag's life. King Saul just didn't listen. That's how the King Saul spirit got King Saul to heed to the final destruction: spiritual, and eventually physical, suicide.

David's repentance:

David, on the other hand, was just as guilty as King Saul, but his repentance was different.

So David said to Nathan, "<u>I have sinned against the Lord.</u>" And Nathan said to David, "The Lord also has put away your sin; you shall not die. However, because by this deed you have given great occasion to the enemies of the Lord to blaspheme, <u>the child also who is born to you shall surely die.</u>"
　　　—2 Samuel 12:13-14, (emphasis mine)

David repented and confessed to God, not to Nathan. Nathan heard David confess and repent, and he knew David was serious. God also knew that David's heart was true, and that he had really repented. This saved David from committing spiritual suicide. This is also why the **Holy Spirit did not depart** from King David, as He did from King Saul. David was forgiven and he knew that he must never commit that sin again. David had a counterattack for the King Saul spirit. It was **true repentance**. The King Saul spirit has no answer for that kind of behavior, my friend. It doesn't know what to do when we truly repent to God. Listen to David's words in the following scripture. Did you ever hear King Saul say this?

　　To the Chief Musician.
　　A Psalm of David when Nathan the prophet went to him, after he had gone in to Bathsheba.
　　<u>Have mercy upon me,</u> O God, according to Your lovingkindness;

> According to the multitude of Your tender
> mercies, <u>blot out my transgressions. Wash me</u>
> thoroughly from my iniquity, and <u>cleanse me
> from my sin.</u>
> For <u>I acknowledge my transgressions,</u>
> and my sin is always before me. Against You,
> <u>You only, have I sinned,</u> and done this evil in
> Your sight, that You may be found just when
> You speak, and blameless when You judge.
> —Psalms 51:1-4, (emphasis mine)

David asked God to change him and clean him up, because he knew he had committed a sin that revealed he was not in God's will. David realized he needed a big change to keep the King Saul spirit out of his life. He realized he needed God to restore him. Remember, earlier on I said that King David's evil behavior was due to disobedience to God's Word. This scripture explains further.

> Create in me a clean heart, O God,
> And renew a steadfast spirit within me.
> Do not cast me away from Your presence,
> <u>And do not take Your Holy Spirit from me.</u>
> <u>Restore to me the joy of Your salvation,</u>
> And uphold me by Your generous Spirit.
> —Psalms 51:10-12, (emphasis mine)

Here we see that David was asking God not to remove him from His presence. He asked God not to take away the Holy Spirit. So David knew that he still had the Holy Spirit. Why doesn't the Holy Spirit leave you when you sin? Well, who's going to convict you of your sin, if the Holy Spirit has left? We need the Holy Spirit to show us where we're going to make a mistake or miss the mark: in other words, where and when we're going to sin. We need the Holy Spirit to tell us, after we've sinned, that we better confess and repent. If you don't listen to the Holy Spirit, but stay in willful sin, oh yes, then there's no doubt that the Holy Spirit eventually can depart from you. Willful sin can get you into big trouble.

> <u>For if we sin willfully</u> after we have received the knowledge of the truth, <u>there no longer remains a sacrifice for sins,</u> but a certain fearful expectation of judgment, and fiery indignation which will devour the adversaries.
> —Hebrews 10:26-27, (emphasis mine)

You see, willful sin takes its toll. King Saul knew the truth. He knew what he had to do. He just never did it. He did things his way, not God's way. He just kept on going back, doing the same sins over and over, and the time came when the Holy Spirit departed from him.

King David responded differently. The moment he realized he was wrong, he came to his senses, repented, and turned away from the sin. That's why the Holy Spirit did not depart from him. The Holy Spirit helped David by urging him to repent.

So David asked God not to take the Holy Spirit away from him. What else did he ask God? That God would restore to him the joy of his salvation. By willful sin we forfeit this joy and deprive ourselves of it. David did not lose the Holy Spirit, like Saul did, but lost the joy of his salvation. I can hear David saying, *"God, please, I have no more joy. I am miserable; I'm sad. Restore my joy back to me."* God did just that. He restored the joy of David's salvation back to him. That's why the King Saul spirit no longer had a hold on King David. David had changed back to the man he had been: the chosen, anointed, Holy Ghost-filled man of God, confessing and repenting of his sins. What a victory over the King Saul spirit!

However, David and Bathsheba's child was going to die as an initial consequence of their sin. David fasted and prayed to God to spare the child. Nevertheless, when the child eventually died, David got up and went on with his life. He knew he had repented. He knew God had forgiven him, and I think he was just glad not ending up being a dead man, like King Saul. David had overcome the King Saul spirit. David knew that repenting and turning away from his sin would stop the advance of the King Saul spirit. You and I can do the same, my dear friend; so come on, it's time we start doing it.

Did God really forgive David and Bathsheba? Oh yes. After the death of the child and the mourning, King David went in to his wife and lay with her again. A new son was born to them nine months later, Solomon. He became the next king, as you know. This was the bloodline of Jesus. God forgives and blesses true **repentance.**

And when He had removed him, He raised up for them David as king, to whom also He gave testimony and said, "I have found David the son of Jesse, a man after My own heart, who will do all My will." <u>From this man's seed</u>, according to the promise, <u>God raised up for Israel a Savior—Jesus.</u>
—Acts 13:22-23, (emphasis mine)

God redeemed something bad for something good, as a result of David's resistance of the King Saul spirit and repentance. True repentance, my friend, always overcomes the King Saul spirit, and it leads to victory.

Summary of this chapter: In conclusion, let's summarize how King David withstood and resisted the King Saul spirit. In the beginning, King David did not open the door to this spirit; he did not fear, nor did he get impatient. He did not get self-willed or prideful. He wasn't disobedient. He never distressed or troubled his people. He never lied, nor did he accuse his friends of doing wrong. He never got jealous, never behaved rebelliously, and never wanted to touch God's anointed and kill them. He was a great man of war and killed the enemy. David was a great man of God.

Nevertheless, he was tricked by the devil, and the door was opened. That's when the King Saul spirit attacked him, and he ended up being just like King Saul. All of a sudden he became disobedient, jealous, deceitful, fearful, and even murderous. Thank the Lord he realized his sin and counterattacked the King

Saul spirit with **true repentance**. David's life was spared, all because he had discerned and overcome the King Saul spirit.

This shows me that when you and I are doing well, and are not being controlled by the King Saul spirit, we still have to watch out for its attack. When it shows up, don't give in and don't give up; we're not doomed. No, fight back; resist this spirit by repentance and confession. God will forgive us. We might still have consequences of our sin, but our spiritual life will be spared. If we don't, we might end up like King Saul, committing suicide.

Get a David spirit in you, adapt a David attitude, and let's overcome the King Saul spirit.

Let's look at another way of counterattacking and neutralizing this King Saul spirit.

CHAPTER 5

From Saul to Paul

—ɯ—

We've been looking at this King Saul spirit in the Old Testament, because that's where it all started. What about the New Testament? Is there any reference to it in there? Well, I immediately thought about Saul, the Pharisee, and a very well-known man to all of us. Saul knew the Scriptures and was a fierce persecutor of Christians.

Another example of how to counterattack and withstand the King Saul spirit can be found in the story of Saul the Pharisee, who is better known as the apostle Paul. Let's find out who Saul the Pharisee was.

Who was Saul?

Saul was born in the city of Tarsus, a big, important city in Cilicia. Saul was a Hebrew, a Jew from the tribe of Benjamin, like King David. Saul was a Pharisee and the son of a Pharisee. He was taught by the best teachers of the law, so he was an intelligent man.

> I am indeed a Jew, born in <u>Tarsus of Cilicia,</u> but brought up in this city at the feet of <u>Gamaliel, taught according to the strictness of our fathers' law,</u> and was zealous toward God as you all are today.
> —Acts 22:3, (emphasis mine)

> ... Circumcised the eighth day, of the <u>stock of Israel,</u> of the <u>tribe of Benjamin,</u> a <u>Hebrew of the Hebrews;</u> concerning the law, <u>a Pharisee.</u>
> —Philippians 3:5, (emphasis mine)

Unfortunately, Saul was being controlled and used by the King Saul spirit. Forget about the fear, impatience, disobedience, self-will, pride, jealousy, deceitfulness, rebellion, and loss of the Holy Spirit. Forget about all these characteristics of the King Saul spirit for now. Saul had been so viciously attacked by the King Saul spirit that he skipped the usual sequence and went right to destruction. He was murdering Christians with all his might. He was persecuting and destroying the church, doing everything in his power to harm believers. I suppose you can say that if he was doing these cruel things to people that he must have had pride in him. He definitely did not have the Holy Spirit in him and he was definitely disobedient to the Word of God, for all the damage he was doing to the Christians. He was probably at least thirty years old and his aim in life was the persecution of the Christian believers.

After Stephen's death and burial, Saul continued his persecution of the church, as we are told again and again. He began ravaging the church, entering house after house, and sending Christians to prison, where they were beaten and tortured. This included men and women.

> As for Saul, he made <u>havoc of the church</u>, entering every house, and dragging off men and women, committing them to <u>prison.</u>
> —Acts 8:3, (emphasis mine)

This he did with the permission of the authorities. He had letters from them allowing him to commit these crimes.

> Then Saul, still breathing <u>threats and murder against the disciples</u> of the Lord, went to the high priest and <u>asked letters from him</u> to the synagogues of Damascus, <u>so that if he found any who were of the Way, whether men or women, he might bring them bound to Jerusalem.</u>
> —Acts 9:1-2, (emphasis mine)

These persecuted people were punished, often in the synagogues. Saul followed them to other cities, too, to get them arrested.

> And I <u>punished them</u> often <u>in every syna-
> gogue</u> and compelled them to blaspheme;
> and being exceedingly enraged against them,
> <u>I persecuted them even to foreign cities.</u>
> —Acts 26:11, (emphasis mine)

Saul the Pharisee even had them killed. The
murderous characteristics of the King Saul spirit
were controlling and using Saul to destroy Christians.
Saul had the same killing spirit as King Saul and
King David. He was attacked by the same King Saul
spirit that attacked the two kings. This spirit saw that
Saul was immediately available to be filled with a
murderous attitude. Saul went right to the serious
stuff.

> I persecuted this Way to the <u>death,</u> binding
> and delivering into prisons both men and
> women.
> —Acts 22:4, (emphasis mine)

> This I also did in Jerusalem, and many of the
> saints I <u>shut up in prison,</u> having received
> authority from the chief priests; and when
> they <u>were put to death,</u> I cast my vote against
> them.
> —Acts 26:10, (emphasis mine)

This was Saul's personal testimony: persecuting
and murdering Christians. Saul became famous for
his pursuit of Christians. Everyone knew about him.
Even in Damascus, Ananias had heard of "how much

harm" he had done to Christ's "saints at Jerusalem" (**Acts 9:13**). Even later on in his years, Saul, who was then called Paul, told people what he had done to the Christians. He tried to destroy the church because of this King Saul spirit.

> For you have heard <u>of my former conduct</u> in Judaism, how I <u>persecuted the church</u> of God beyond measure and <u>tried to destroy it.</u>
> —Galatians 1:13, (emphasis mine)

Summary of this chapter: Saul was a Pharisee, who was taught the law and knew the Scriptures. He must have taught the law, because that's what Pharisees did. He was like the preachers we have today, people who know the Word and teach it to other people. Today we have Christians who know the Word of God, too. Some teach Sunday school; some minister in song; and some are intercessors. Some prophesy and give people a Word from God. Some are preachers and preach in churches. It doesn't matter who you are or what you do in the church. When the King Saul spirit attacks, it can attack anyone and use anyone. As long as it can attack, it can kill and destroy.

Obviously, the King Saul spirit wanted to do the same to Saul as it had done to King Saul. It eventually would have harmed and killed Saul, too, through suicide. Why? Well, because that's the main aim of this King Saul spirit, remember? It wants to get you and me to the point where we commit suicide, whether spiritually or physically. You must remember this.

CHAPTER 6

The Change in Saul

—✺—

The change in Saul was not a bad change. It was a good change. Saul got rid of that King Saul spirit and traded it for the Holy Spirit. What a change! He overcame and defeated the King Saul spirit. How did it happen? Well, Saul was on his way to Damascus to persecute the Christians again, when he had an encounter with God Almighty. Remember, Saul knew about God, but had no relationship with God. I want you to take note of what I've just said. We'll get back to this point again. He had no relationship with God, although he had knowledge of God. Let's see what happened.

As he journeyed he came near Damascus, and suddenly <u>a light shone around him</u> from heaven. Then he fell to the ground, and heard a voice saying to him, "Saul, Saul, why are you persecuting Me?" And he said, "Who are You, Lord?" Then the Lord said, "I am Jesus, whom you are persecuting. It is hard for you to kick against the goads." So he, trembling and astonished, said, "<u>Lord, what do You want me to do?</u>" Then the Lord said to him, "Arise and go into the city, and you will be told what you must do." And the men who journeyed with him stood speechless, hearing a voice but seeing no one. Then Saul arose from the ground, and when his eyes were opened he saw no one. But they led him by the hand and brought him into Damascus. And he was three days without sight, and neither ate nor drank.

—Acts 9:3-9, (emphasis mine)

God shone His light on Saul and he became blind. God spoke to him. God challenged him to stop persecuting His church. Saul asked God what he should do. For the next three days, he ate and drank nothing. I don't think I would want to eat or drink anything either, if I had just had this encounter with God. Saul knew God had pulled his file. Saul had experienced a huge change in his spiritual life. He was about to let go of the King Saul spirit and receive the Holy Spirit. So God sent a disciple, Ananias, to go and pray for Saul. Ananias went, and after he had prayed, Saul received the Holy Ghost and was a changed man . . . a new man, without the King Saul spirit.

But the Lord said to [Ananias], "Go, for he is a <u>chosen</u> vessel of Mine to bear My name before Gentiles, kings, and the children of Israel. For I will show him how many things he must suffer for My name's sake." And Ananias went his way and entered the house; <u>and laying his hands on him</u> he said, "Brother Saul, the Lord Jesus, who appeared to you on the road as you came, has sent me that you may receive your sight and be <u>filled with the Holy Spirit.</u>" Immediately there fell from his eyes something like scales, <u>and he received his sight at once; and he arose and was baptized.</u>

—Acts 9:15-18, (emphasis mine)

Saul was **chosen** by God, just like King Saul, King David, and you and I. God was going to use Saul and keep the King Saul spirit from using him. Nevertheless, Saul still had to make the choice, to accept God's calling and step away from the murderous King Saul spirit to a Holy Ghost-filled life. Thank the Lord he made the right choice. Saul received his sight back, got up, and ate. From that day on Saul was no longer a murderer of the saints. He became a child of God. He became born-again, and the King Saul spirit was defeated. It lost its hold on Saul. What happened? You see, my friend, the moment God's light shone on Saul, it all happened. I believe that if we can stay under the light of God, then the King Saul spirit cannot come near us. God is light, and if we abide in Him, no demon spirit can use and control us.

This is the message which we have heard from Him and declare to you, that <u>God is light</u> and in Him is no darkness at all. . . .But if we walk in the light as He is in the light, we have fellowship with one another, and the blood of Jesus Christ His Son cleanses us from all sin.

—1 John 1:5, 7, (emphasis mine)

Again, a new commandment I write to you, which thing is true in Him and in you, because the darkness is passing away, and the true light is already shining. <u>He, who says he is in the light, and hates his brother,</u> is in darkness until now. He who loves his brother abides in the light, and there is no cause for stumbling in him. But he who hates his brother is in darkness and walks in darkness, and does not know where he is going, because the darkness has blinded his eyes.

—1 John 2:8-11, (emphasis mine)

As you've just read, when we love each other, we are in the light. When we hate each other, we are in darkness. When we love each other, my friend, we won't want to kill and spear each other, or even harm each other. When we're in darkness and hate, we will do harm to others. Remember, when you hate your brother, God says you're a murderer. So it's important to stay in God, in the light, in love, so that we can counterattack and not allow this King Saul spirit to control us.

Whoever <u>hates his brother is a murderer,</u> and you know that no murderer has eternal life abiding in him.

 — 1 John 3:15, (emphasis mine)

The light blinded Saul so that he became literally blind. Saul could not see his old friends or the world out there, until God touched him and made him new. If you and I could only stay in the light, in God, so that we can become blind as well. Blind to what? Well, blind to doing evil, blind to our old friends, and the old way of living. Saul became blind and could not see the world outside anymore. He couldn't see his friends. He could only experience God. That's the key to overcoming this King Saul spirit. We need to become blind to the fear, impatience, self-will, pride, disobedience, rebellion, deceitfulness, and false accusations. We need to become blind to jealousy and spear throwing, trying to kill others. We need to be blind toward hurting our friends and fellow Christians. We need to be in the light, so we can love each other. When you're blind to these characteristics of the King Saul spirit, you won't want to exercise or implement them. You won't want to allow them to affect and control you. All you'll want to do is love and forgive. The King Saul spirit will have a hard time trapping you, controlling your thought life, or using you to destroy and kill your fellow Christians. It definitely won't be able to deceive you to the point of spiritual suicide and backsliding.

Well, Saul then asked God, *"What do you want me to do, Lord?"* That's our next step in neutralizing

185

this King Saul spirit. What does God want us to do? If we have this attitude, we won't get caught up in doing the will of the King Saul spirit; we'll be caught up in doing the **will of God.** This is very important. Why? Well, Saul did not have a relationship with God. Although he had all the knowledge about God, he never knew God. Many times there are Christians who know about God. They've prayed the prayer of salvation, but they don't have a relationship with God. The King Saul spirit finds an open door to infiltrate their lives, attacks them, and uses them. That's what happened to Saul, the Pharisee.

Maybe that's one of the great reasons why there are so many Christians being attacked by this King Saul spirit. They've been assigned by this evil spirit to kill their fellow Christians, to split up the church of God, and to commit suicide in the end. They're not walking in the light, although they think they are. They've not become blind to the things of the world, which only occurs when one's focus is on God alone. They definitely don't have a relationship with the Lord Jesus, and they're not asking God what to do. They're following the King Saul spirit and not the Holy Spirit.

Let's carry on. Then Saul was prayed for; he was made new and whole. He received his sight and was prepared to be taught by the disciples. He had to give up his old way of thinking. As Christians, if we want to stop the work of the King Saul spirit, we'll have to do the same thing. We'll have to be prepared to change our way of thinking and do things according the Word of God, not according to the way of the King Saul spirit. We'll have to stop the fear, impatience, pride, disobedience, jealousy, rebellion, deceit, troubling, distress, and false accusation of the brothers. We'll have to repent and turn around. We'll have to stop the murderous spear throwing. We'll have to stop gossiping, criticizing, and judging people. We'll have to forgive and love with the love of the Lord. No more splitting up churches. No more murdering the saints of God. No more backsliding. No more spiritual suicide.

It's time to change and live according to God's Word. We'll have to come into the light of God, and be the light of God. We'll have to become blind to the things of the world and live righteous, powerful Christian lives. My friend, we'll have to do it God's way and be prepared to be taught righteousness by the Holy Spirit. That's the only way we're going to overcome and counterattack this King Saul spirit.

The difference in Saul was very obvious. After his conversion, he started preaching the gospel of Jesus Christ. Previously he was a murderer of Christians. He immediately turned around and preached the Christ. Saul had counterattacked the enemy, the King Saul spirit. We'll have to adapt the same attitude. We'll have to start preaching Jesus to the people and bring them the good news. We'll have to start restoring what we've broken, just as Saul did. Saul became Paul, from the bad to the good, from "Saul to Paul."

Then Saul, who also is called Paul, filled with the Holy Spirit, looked intently at him

and said, "O full of all deceit and all fraud, you son of the devil, you enemy of all righteousness, will you not cease perverting the straight ways of the Lord?"
— Acts 13:9-10, (emphasis mine)

Saul had become Paul, filled with the Holy Spirit. Paul became one of the most influential preachers of the gospel of Jesus. God gave him all the revelation to write most of the epistles of the New Testament. He started driving out demons, healing the sick, and doing unusual miracles **(Acts 19:11-12).** Wow, what a change, from a murderer to a miracle worker! He raised people from the dead. Paul prophesied over many people. Paul had the relationship with God that you and I should have. God took a murderer of the Christians and made him a witness for Jesus to the world. Paul's work still is influencing and training us today. We should pay attention to this man, who was able to get rid of the King Saul spirit.

Now God worked unusual miracles by the hands of Paul, so that even handkerchiefs or aprons were brought from his body to the sick, and the diseases left them and the evil spirits went out of them.
— Acts 19:11-12, (emphasis mine)

Scripture after scripture tells us of how Paul testified and witnessed. Paul was turned around, from a *murderer to* a *preacher.* If God can do that for Paul, then God can turn us away from murdering our fellow

Christians and make us witnesses, too. We can do exactly what Paul did. You see, instead of focusing on destroying the church and the Christians, Paul focused on healing and loving his fellow Christians and building the church. What a difference! Let's take Paul as an example and change our lives around from hurting people to loving them. You see, your mouth was not given to you to destroy people. It was given to you to praise God, to speak the word of God, to testify about Jesus. It was given to us to build up, not to break down and destroy. It was given to us to edify people.

Summary of this chapter: We can stop this murderous King Saul spirit. We don't have to be controlled and used by it. We don't have to be attacked by it. We can be free from its bondage. Let's be set free; let's turn around from being a "Saul" and become a "Paul." Let's defeat and neutralize this King Saul spirit like the apostle Paul did.

PART THREE

LIVING WITHOUT THE KING SAUL SPIRIT

—⁂—

CHAPTER 1

Kill the King Saul Spirit

—⚬—

W hat do we do when we identify the King Saul spirit? We kill it. We destroy it and neutralize it. We fight fire with fire. This King Saul spirit is a killing, destroying spirit, so we kill and destroy it before it kills and destroys us or our churches. Let's talk a bit of Texan English.

> ### *"Kill the King Saul spirit before it kills ya'll's spirit."*

That's sounds good to me, how about you? If you don't kill the King Saul spirit, it will eventually kill **your spirit;** that's a fact.

My dear friend, we can't afford to play around with this spirit. We can't allow it to use and control our lives. It's too dangerous. We have to get rid of it and destroy it quickly and completely.

Well, there are a few things we can do. It just depends on when, where, and how you identify it.

We must realize that the King Saul spirit is only a name for a group of individual demonic spirits, working together. The devil is taking certain spirits and using them to destroy us, as we allow him to. I have mentioned all the characteristics of the King Saul spirit in previous chapters, but these characteristics are really individual demonic spirits. They are grouped together by the devil and used as a force to destroy God's church and His people. I've called this demonic force the King Saul spirit.

Let's recap these characteristics, or individual spirits: the spirit of fear, the spirit of impatience, the spirit of pride, the spirit of disobedience or rebellion, the spirit of distress and trouble, the spirit of lying or deceitfulness, the spirit of false accusations, the spirit of jealousy, and the spirit of murder or spear throwing. This murderous spirit also may be known as the spirit of gossip, criticism, judgment, or even murder, destruction, and suicide. All of these individual spirits, often working together as a group in a sequence, we call the King Saul spirit.

How can we live a victorious life free from these spirits? How do we kill, destroy, and neutralize them in our lives and our churches? Well, I'm not going to go into too much detail, but I'm going to give you some Scriptures and advice on how we can get rid of them.

How do we deal with these spirits when they show up? What I'm going to explain might sound easier than it really is. I'm not going to lie to you; it's not easy, but it's worthwhile and we can do it. We'll just have to persevere in the fight of faith to overcome them. We have all the weapons available, but we have to use them and never give up.

CHAPTER 2

Dealing With Individual Spirits

—〰—

1) **The spirit of fear**: Everyone has had some kind of fear attacking them, right? Well, God says you don't have to be afraid. When the devil puts fear in you, you have to retaliate through your faith in God. You'll have to say, *"No, devil, I will not fear, I'm going to trust God to help me. I'm putting my faith in God; my confidence, my assurance, and my reliance is in God. He will get me through this fight. I will not fear."* This is the only way you must speak and think. Remember the devil wants you to worry when you're in fear. Fear is basically laid out as *False Evidence Appearing Real.* Faith is not false: *it is the substance of things hoped for, the evidence of things not seen* **(Heb. 11:1).** You're not to be moved by the false evidence you can see; you're to be moved by the things you know, what the Word of God says is true. You function according to the Word of God, nothing

else. Here are some scriptures that you can quote when fear attacks you. You'll have to keep these words in your mouth all day long. When the attack comes, you can say, "I will not fear." Why? Well, because God's Word says I should not fear, that's why. Speak these scriptures daily.

For God <u>has not given us a spirit of fear,</u> but of power and of love and of a sound mind.
　　　　　　—2 Timothy 1:7, (emphasis mine)

A Psalm of David.
The Lord is my light and my salvation;
<u>Whom shall I fear?</u>
The Lord is the strength of my life;
<u>Of whom shall I be afraid</u>?
　　　　　　—Psalms 27:1, (emphasis mine)

The Lord is on my side;
<u>I will not fear</u>.
What can man do to me?
　　　　　　—Psalms 118:6, (emphasis mine)

You shall <u>not be afraid of the terror by night</u>,
Nor of the arrow that flies by day,
For He shall give His angels charge over you,
To keep you in all your ways.
　　　　　　—Psalms 91:5, 11, (emphasis mine)

Yea, though I walk through the valley of the
    shadow of death,
I will fear no evil; For You are with me;
Your rod and Your staff, they comfort me.
           —Psalms 23:4, (emphasis mine)

Fear not, for I am with you;
Be not dismayed, for I am your God.
I will strengthen you,
Yes, I will help you,
I will uphold you with My righteous right hand.
           —Isaiah 41:10, (emphasis mine)

There is no fear in love; but perfect love casts
out fear, because fear involves torment. But he
who fears has not been made perfect in love.
           —1 John 4:18, (emphasis mine)

My friend there are many more scriptures you can find in the Word. The bottom line is you don't have to fear. When you sense fear rising up in you, you can overcome it. You have the Word of God to use against it. Speak that Word to the fear spirit, in the powerful name of Jesus Christ.

2) **The spirit of impatience:** I'm sure all of us have been impatient some time or another in our lives. How do you stop the spirit of impatience? Well, you have to change your mind-set to be more patient. Is that easy? Oh no, definitely not. You'll have to walk in the Spirit to be able to be patient.

Patience is part of the fruit of the Spirit. Only the Holy Spirit can help you and me to be patient. When you feel impatient, you'll have to make a decision that you're not going to allow this spirit to take control of you. You'll have to ask the Holy Spirit to help you replace the spirit of impatience with patience. You know why the devil wants you to be impatient, right? It always leads to trouble. You and I don't need that kind of trouble; we need to be patient, so we can be blessed—that's much better. Say it out loud: *"I will not be impatient; I will do what the Word says and be patient. I will walk in the Spirit and let the fruit of the Spirit flow through me. I will be patient in Jesus' name."* So let's look at some scriptures that we can quote when we're attacked by the spirit of impatience.

That you do not become sluggish, but imitate those who through <u>faith and patience</u> inherit the promises.

—Hebrews 6:12, (emphasis mine)

My brethren, count it all joy when you fall into various trials, knowing that <u>the testing of your faith produces patience.</u> But <u>let patience have its perfect work,</u> that you may be perfect and complete, lacking nothing.

—James 1:2-4, (emphasis mine)

And a servant of the Lord must not quarrel but be gentle to all, able to teach, <u>patient.</u>

—2 Timothy 2:24, (emphasis mine)

The King Saul Spirit

But you, O man of God, flee these things and pursue righteousness, godliness, faith, love, <u>paticnce,</u> gentleness.
— 1 Timothy 6:11, (emphasis mine)

Don't let impatience rule you; be a patient believer. Once again, use the Word of God to help you. Ask the Holy Spirit for strength and let the fruit of the Spirit flow out of you. Make these Scriptures personal, and say; "I am a man or woman of God, I will pursue righteousness, godliness, faith, love patience and gentleness." Do this with all the Scriptures I've given you.

3) **<u>The spirit of pride and of being self-willed:</u>** My fellow believer, I have to warn you that the devil wants you to become prideful, because God hates pride. **Prov.6: 16, 17;** *these six things the LORD hates, yes, seven are an abomination to Him: A <u>proud look</u>, a lying tongue, Hands that shed innocent blood.* (emphasis mine)
Pride was the reason the devil himself was kicked out of heaven, remember? He wants you to be kept out of heaven, too.

Not a novice, lest being puffed up with <u>pride he fall</u> into the same condemnation <u>as the devil.</u>
— 1 Timothy 3:6, (emphasis mine)

This spirit will make you fall.

201

First pride, then the crash, the bigger the ego,
the harder the fall.
—Proverbs 16:18 MESSAGE, (emphasis mine)

Pride goes before destruction,
And a haughty spirit before a fall.
—Proverbs 16:18, (emphasis mine)

The Lord will destroy the house of the
proud,
But He will establish the boundary of the
widow.
—Proverbs 15:25, (emphasis mine)

So how do we get pride out of the way? We fight pride by being humble, my friend. That's one of the greatest weapons we have for neutralizing pride. Why? Pride says, *"I'll do it my way."* To be humble means: *"The subjection of our will to God's will, regardless of how we feel, or the circumstances we're in. Not my will, but Thy will be done."* Once again, we'll have to ask the Holy Spirit to help us to stay humble. We'll have to adapt the attitude David had when he asked God to help him, in the scripture mentioned below. Let's look at some other scriptures as well, which we can use to withstand the spirit of pride.

Let not the foot of pride come against me,
And let not the hand of the wicked drive
me away. [This was David's request to the
Lord.]
—Psalms 36:11, (emphasis mine)

If My people who are called by My name will humble themselves, and pray and seek My face, and turn from their wicked ways, then I will hear from heaven, and will forgive their sin and heal their land.
  —2 Chronicles 7:14, (emphasis mine)

Likewise you younger people, submit yourselves to your elders. Yes, all of you be submissive to one another, and be clothed with humility, for "God resists the proud, But gives grace to the humble." Therefore humble yourselves under the mighty hand of God, that He may exalt you in due time, casting all your care upon Him, for He cares for you.
  —1 Peter 5:5-7, (emphasis mine)

For whoever exalts himself will be humbled, and he who humbles himself will be exalted.
  —Luke 14:11, (emphasis mine)

By humility and the fear of the Lord are riches and honor and life.
  —Proverbs 22:4, (emphasis mine)

You will save the humble people;
But Your eyes are on the haughty [prideful], that You may bring them down.
  —Samuel 22:28, (emphasis mine)

You have to resist this pride spirit. The problem is that most of us don't even realize when we're in pride. So get someone to help you. Someone you can be accountable to, who can tell you when you're being prideful. Someone you trust, who can speak into your life as soon as they identify such behavior. It might not be easy to handle, but it's worth it.

After reading these scriptures, I don't know about you, but I don't want to be caught up in a pride trap. I'd rather stay humble and submit to God. We can defeat the spirit of pride.

4) **The spirit of disobedience or rebellion:** Can we get rid of this kind of spirit? Of course we can. This is an easy one, if we just follow the instructions in God's Word. *Disobedience is a key to failure.* So the only way to overcome it is through obedience. *Obedience is the key to success.* Everywhere in the Word we can recognize the promises of God, if we're obedient. My friend, every time we step into disobedience, we know it, right? There's always that little something that's not right . . . that's bothering you. I've made many mistakes not listening to those inner warnings from the Holy Spirit, that small little voice warning me. We'll have to condition our minds to be obedient. We'll have to decide that we are going to do what the Word of God says and not listen to the word of the enemy. Get these scriptures into your heart and do them. Do the Word of God and be blessed as you defeat the spirit of disobedience and rebellion.

If you are willing and <u>obedient,</u>
You shall eat the good of the land.
>   —Isaiah 1:19, (emphasis mine)

    If they <u>obey and serve Him,</u>
    They shall spend their days in <u>prosperity, (wealth, favour, goodness, being well). And their years in pleasures.</u>
>   —Job 36:11, (emphasis mine)

Now it shall come to pass, if you diligently <u>obey the voice</u> of the Lord your God, to observe carefully all His commandments which I command you today, that the Lord your God will set you high above all nations of the earth. And all these <u>blessings shall come upon</u> you and overtake you, <u>because you obey the voice</u> of the Lord your God.
>   —Deuteronomy 28:1-2, (emphasis mine)

Look at these blessings:

1. You will be blessed in the city (<u>Deut. 28:3</u>).
2. You will be blessed in the field.
3. You will have perfect offspring (<u>Deut. 28:4</u>).
4. Your crops will be blessed.
5. Your cattle will increase.
6. Your flocks will increase.
7. Your baskets and storehouses will be full of good things (<u>Deut. 28:5, 8</u>).
8. You will be blessed in all you undertake (<u>Deut. 28:6, 8</u>).

9. You will have complete victory over all your enemies (<u>Deut. 28:7</u>).
10. Your land will be abundantly fertile and productive.
11. You will be established as a holy people to God (<u>Deut. 28:9</u>).
12. You will be a witness and an example to all people on earth (<u>Deut. 28:10</u>).
13. All nations will be afraid of you.
14. You will be prosperous in goods, in children, in stock, and in crops in all the land (<u>Deut. 28:11</u>).
15. The Lord will open to you all His good treasure (<u>Deut. 28:12</u>).
16. The heavens will give you rain in due season in all your land.
17. The Lord will bless all the work of your hands.
18. You will be prosperous enough to lend to many nations, and you will not need to borrow from them.
19. The Lord shall make you the head, and not the tail (<u>Deut. 28:13</u>).
20. You shall be above all men and never beneath them.

The whole idea of being obedient is that God wants to bless you when you are obedient to Him. That will neutralize the spirit of disobedience and please God.

5) <u>**The spirit of lying:**</u> This is another aspect of the King Saul spirit that God hates. **Prov.6: 16, 17;** *these six things the LORD hates, yes, seven are an*

abomination to Him: A proud look, <u>a lying tongue</u>, Hands that shed innocent blood. (emphasis mine). He hates lying. Why? Well, because the devil is the father of lies. Jesus told the Pharisees in **John 8:44:** *"You are of your father the devil, and the desires of your father you want to do. He was a murderer from the beginning, <u>and does not stand in the truth</u>, because <u>there is no truth in him. When he speaks a lie</u>, he speaks from his own resources, <u>for he is a liar and the father of it"</u>* (emphasis mine). God has made it clear that **lying** does not originate from Him. It comes from the devil himself. The Word says that it's impossible for God to lie. **Hebrews 6:18:** *"That by two immutable things, <u>in which it is impossible for God to lie,</u> we might have strong consolation, who have fled for refuge to lay hold of the hope set before us"* (emphasis mine). Why is lying so bad? Well, it could make you go to hell, did you know? It's not something to play with. **Revelation 21:8:** *"But the cowardly, unbelieving, abominable, murderers, sexually immoral, sorcerers, idolaters, and <u>all liars</u> shall have their part in the lake which burns with fire and brimstone, which is the second death"* (emphasis mine).

The only way to counterattack the lying spirit is to make sure you always tell the truth. We must never lie. Walk in the truth. Don't try and impress people by telling a story that's not true; it only will catch up with you, and you'll be found out. Most people don't like other people lying to them, but still they lie themselves. Make sure that you never exaggerate. You don't have to be ashamed of what you have or what happened; tell the truth, that's what set's you free, remember? *"And you shall know the truth, and the truth shall make you free"* **(John 8:32).** Lying gets you into trouble; the truth sets you free. Let the devil know that you're finished listening to his lies and he's not going to control you through his lies anymore. Make an effort to stay in the truth and stop lying. John said in **3 John 1:3-4,** *"For I rejoiced greatly when brethren came and testified of the truth that is in you, just as you walk in the truth. I have no greater joy than to hear that my children walk in truth"* (emphasis mine). As born-again believers, we should not lie to each other. *"Do not lie to one another, since you have put off the old man with his deeds"* **(Col. 3:9)** (emphasis mine). Let's get this lying spirit neutralized and get him out of our lives. Let's start walking in the **truth,** in Jesus, who said in **John 14:6,** *"Jesus said to him, 'I am the way, the truth, and the life. No one comes to the Father except through Me.'"* We'll have to tell ourselves, *"I will speak the truth, I will not lie. God hates lying. It's not good for me; it can get me into trouble. I am a man of truth: I only speak the truth, the Word of God. I will not listen to the father of lies, the devil. I will listen and do what Jesus said, the One who is the truth. I will not lie to people because I am a new man; I have put off the deeds of the old man."* Remember for every one lie that you tell, you have to tell five more lies to cover up the first one. The more you lie, the more you have to lie to try and get out of trouble. It's not worth it.

6) **The spirit of jealousy:** How do we overcome this spirit? We have to remember that jealousy comes from comparing things in your life, to things in others' lives. God knew this would cause **jealousy,** so He stated that we should not compare ourselves to each other. *"For <u>we dare not class ourselves or compare ourselves</u> with those who commend themselves. But they, measuring themselves by themselves, <u>and comparing themselves among themselves</u>, <u>are not wise"</u>* (**2 Cor. 10:12**) (emphasis mine). We get rid of this spirit with an attitude of: no comparisons. Some might wonder if jealousy is really a spirit, or a feeling. It's a spirit. *"Or when <u>the spirit of jealousy</u> comes upon a man, and he becomes jealous of his wife; then he shall stand the woman before the Lord, and the priest shall execute all this law upon her"* (**Num. 5:30**) (emphasis mine). Jealousy is a spirit; the Word confirms it. This spirit is dangerous as well. *"Wrath is cruel and anger a torrent, but who is able to stand before <u>jealousy?"</u>* (**Prov. 27:4**) (emphasis mine). God's view on jealousy is that He does not want us to live that way. *"Let us walk properly, as in the day, not in revelry and drunkenness, not in lewdness and lust, not in strife and <u>envy</u> - <u>(jealousy)</u>."* (**Romans 13:13**) (emphasis mine). He says we're living carnal, or just like the worldly people when we're acting in jealousy. *"For you are still carnal. For where there are*

envy, or (jealousy), strife, and divisions among you, are you not carnal and behaving like mere men?" (**1 Corinthians 3:3**) (emphasis mine).

You see, people who are wise and pure aren't jealous. Why? Well, they're glad when someone else has done well. When someone else is blessed, they rejoice with them, because they know that their blessing is on the way soon. They praise God with the people who are blessed. They would not be jealous and envious. We have to realize that jealousy is not godly. Let's share in other people's happiness, in what they have, instead of envying them. Share in their excitement, and we'll defeat the spirit of jealousy. Your turn will come; just be patient and wait for God to bless you too. Tell this spirit of jealousy to go. Tell it to leave in Jesus' name. It has no right to attack you and hurt you. Tell it that you will not give in to its control over your life. Defeat this spirit by saying, *"I don't compare other people's blessings to mine; I share in other people's happiness. I will not act carnal, I will not be like the world, and I will walk and resist the spirit of jealousy, in Jesus' name."* Remember, this jealousy spirit, if not neutralized, can lead to you and me killing our fellow Christians,

7) **The murdering spirit of spear throwing:** Out of all the spirits discussed so far, I think this is one of the most vicious, but important, spirits to overcome. God does not want us to spear each other with spears of gossip, criticism, or judgment. We have to stop killing the anointed of

God. How? Let me ask you this. How many of us like it when people criticize us, or gossip about us, or even judge us? No one likes it, right? So then, why are *we* still doing it? If we don't like others doing it to us, we should stop doing it to them. Unforgiveness, hurt, anger, resentment, hatred, and backbiting will disappear when we decide that we're not going to throw these spears anymore, but focus on loving our brothers and sisters. Most of the spearing is done through the words we speak, words that destroy people's lives. Love will not allow that. *"Yes, but they've hurt me, so I've got to retaliate,"* you might say. No, if you love them, love will cover that sin. *"And above all things have fervent love for one another, for 'love will cover a multitude of sins'"* **(1 Pet. 4:8)** (emphasis mine).

God wants us to love, not to hate and kill. That's how we're going to defeat this killing spirit, my friend, through love. Decide to change your way of speaking and say, *"I will not speak evil of my neighbor; I will not gossip and criticize them. I will not judge them or harm them. I will not do anything that can hurt or spiritually kill my neighbor. I will love them with the love of God and forgive them if they've wronged me."* Then we have to live that way, too. People, who love, don't want to gossip, criticize, judge or speak evil of their fellow Christians. They see no need of it; it's foolish to act like that. This is how we're going to reverse the killing spears we've thrown at our anointed brothers and sisters. Start believing, speaking, and acting out these scriptures.

> And the second is like it: "You <u>shall love your neighbor</u> as yourself."
> —Matthew 22:39, (emphasis mine)

> This is My commandment, <u>that you love one another</u> as I have loved you.
> —John 15:12, (emphasis mine)

> Beloved, <u>let us love one another,</u> for love is of God; and everyone who loves is born of God and knows God.
> —1 John 4:7, (emphasis mine)

> And this commandment we have from Him: that <u>he who loves God must love his brother also.</u>
> —1 John 4:21, (emphasis mine)

> <u>Hatred stirs up strife, but love covers all sins.</u>
> —Proverbs 10:12, (emphasis mine)

Love, my friends, is the only answer against this killing spirit, and we'll have to start implementing this love of God toward our fellow Christians.

8) **The suicide spirit:** This is the most dangerous and destructive spirit to deal with. This is the ultimate goal of the King Saul spirit. This is the

spirit that wants you to kill yourself. It wants you to commit spiritual suicide, and in many cases, even physical death can occur. How do we deal with this kind of spirit? First of all, why would you want to kill your own spiritual life? What happens in a person's mind that makes him too blind to see that what he's doing to others also is harming him? Well, when someone is totally controlled and used by the King Saul spirit, they become so helpless that they go to the world for help. That's when they backslide and turn from God. This happens when a person has given in to one or more, if not all, of the previously mentioned spirits. So the only way to get rid of the suicide spirit is to make sure you don't allow any of the above mentioned spirits to control and use you. If you can deal with these spirits individually, it's much easier to overcome them. The moment you allow them to group together and team up against you, they become more difficult to conquer.

You and I will have to ask God to help us, so that we can identify these spirits individually. By the time the King Saul spirit has trapped us, so that we want to commit *spiritual suicide,* most of us are very ashamed of ourselves. Most of us feel so rejected and unworthy that we don't believe the church loves us anymore. Most of the people that are hurt don't even believe God loves them anymore. They don't believe God will forgive them, and they become hopeless.

I think the best way to deal with the suicide spirit is to stop, think, and realize that God is still faithful.

God never changes. If we'll come back to God—repent, confess, and turn away from our sin—God will take us back and forgive us. That's what Jesus died for.

> If <u>we confess our sins</u>, He is faithful and just <u>to forgive us our sins</u> and to cleanse us from all unrighteousness.
>
> —1 John 1:9, (emphasis mine)

We have to remember this, or else we'll stay bound up by this suicide spirit and kill ourselves. We have to remember that God loves us, and His grace and mercy is always available for us. We have to get out of the willful sin and truly confess and repent, and we'll be forgiven. Don't listen to the lies of the devil, telling you you're not good enough: *God won't forgive you; you're too bad; you've done wrong; and nobody cares for you anymore.* No, that's not true. If you truly repent as David and Paul did, God will give you a second chance. So why should God forgive us, after all that we've done wrong? Remember, we are chosen by God, we're anointed by God. We have the Holy Spirit. God's with us. God loves us and has given us a new heart. He has changed us. We're special people to God. We're accepted by God. Let me give you some scriptures to remind you of this truth.

> But you are a <u>chosen generation,</u> a <u>royal priesthood,</u> a <u>holy nation,</u> His own <u>special people,</u> that you may proclaim the praises of

Him who called you out of darkness into His
marvelous light.
>   — 1 Peter 2:9, emphasis mine

To the praise of the glory of His grace, by
which He has made us <u>accepted in the</u>
<u>Beloved.</u>
>   —Ephesians 1:6, emphasis mine

I will praise You, for <u>I am fearfully</u> and
<u>wonderfully made;</u>
<u>Marvelous</u> are Your works,
And that my soul knows very well.
>   —Psalms 139:14, emphasis mine

Know who you are in Christ and turn away from
the sin you've committed. Return to your God and be
forgiven. Get out of the world and come back home
to your family and your God. Don't let this King Saul
spirit *kill your spirit*. Don't let it deceive you into
killing yourself. The Word says in **Philippians 4:13,**
*"I can do all things through Christ who strengthens
me."* So, if that's true, then I'm sure we can defeat
and kill the King Saul spirit.

CHAPTER 3

Getting Help and Helping Others

—〰—

When you realize that you've been attacked and are being used by this King Saul spirit, and you identify that it's working in you, what are you going to do? I suggest that the first thing you do is **repent**. Ask **God to forgive** you, and then **make right with the people** you've harmed. Ask them **to forgive you**. Get help from someone who can **pray with you** and deliver you from this murderous King Saul spirit. Go to your pastor or a spiritual counselor. You need to **renounce** all the hatred and fear, all the disobedience and lying, and all the pride and jealousy. You need to stop throwing spears of gossip and criticism. You have to stop the judgment and rebellion. You'll have to stop spreading false accusations about people. You'll have to stop the destruction in other people's lives. Only God can forgive you and me and set us free, so let's ask Him to do it. If you need any other kind of spiritual help, please go and get it.

Then, be careful that this King Saul spirit doesn't get another open door in your life. If and when you see these characteristics coming back, stop right there and repeat the process. **Confess** and **repent** immediately; call your prayer partners or spiritual friends and ask for prayer. You cannot afford for this thing to come back into your life. It will come back seven times worse. Ask God what to do so you can help yourself. Then walk in love, as God wants us to. Stay in the Holy Spirit, stay in the Word of God. Put on the whole armor of God and protect yourself with the blood of Jesus. Be a light to the world and heal people and the church, rather than destroy them. You have the Holy Ghost power to be a victor, not a loser. You can overcome this King Saul spirit by the blood of Jesus and by the word of your testimony. Do it!

And they overcame him by the blood of the Lamb and by the word of their testimony, and they did not love their lives to the death.
—Revelation 12:11, (emphasis mine)

What do you do when you identify the King Saul spirit in the person next to you? Well, you really cannot walk up to them and say, *"Hey, you're being used by an evil spirit called the **King Saul spirit,** and you're a bad person."* No, you can't do that. So what can you do?

I suggest the first thing you do is **pray** for those people. They desperately need your prayers. Don't tell other people what you've identified. Don't start talking evil about these people behind their backs. This will only make you as guilty as they are, and you'll be acting just like the King Saul spirit wants you to. Before you know it, you'll be used and attacked by it, and you'll be destroying lives as well. No, you pray for and minister to them. You explain to them what the Word says when you get the chance. All you can do is just love them and show them the right way to handle the situation. Remember, they'll try and get you involved in their little game, and you'll know when this King Saul spirit shows up. So, is this all you can do to help them?

No, you also can confide in the spiritual leader of the church, the pastor. You can go to him and tell him what you've seen and indentified. Let's say you're in the worship team, and things aren't going too well because one of the other singers that's being used by the King Saul spirit. Go see your pastor and tell him the situation. Then let the pastor handle it, not you.

You're not in charge; you can only pray for them. That's the best thing you can do.

So if you think you've been controlled and used by this King Saul spirit, what and how can you get free from it? I would suggest that you pray the following prayer; it will help you to renounce this spirit.

Father, I recognize and admit that I have been entertaining this King Saul spirit in my life. So I'm asking You in the name of Jesus, to forgive me for allowing this King Saul spirit to control and use me. Forgive me if

I've harmed my friends, fellow believers, my church, or myself. I repent and confess, Lord, of listening to the lies of this spirit and doing what it told me to do. Forgive me, Lord, for letting fear, impatience, pride, disobedience, self-will, and deceitfulness control me. I'm sorry for distressing and troubling my friends and falsely accusing them. I'm sorry for acting foolishly and becoming jealous of my fellow believers. Forgive me, Father, for throwing spears of gossip, criticism, and judgment at my Christian brothers and sisters. Lord, I'm sorry for wanting to destroy and hurt them. I did not even know I was doing it. Forgive me, Lord. Father, I'm asking You to forgive me for allowing the spirit of suicide in my life. I am sorry for letting this King Saul spirit almost destroy me through spiritual suicide. I thank You for Your forgiveness, for the blood that washes me clean from my sin, right now. I accept my forgiveness and my spiritual healing. Restore the joy of my salvation, Lord, as I give my heart to You, anew afresh. Thank You that I'm Your child and You're my Father. Holy Spirit, please help me not to make the same mistakes again. In Jesus' name I pray, Amen.

Well, there are many ways to pray to God about this. This is just a suggestion. If you've prayed this prayer, God has forgiven you and you're on your way to recovery. Now go and don't allow this King

Saul spirit to control and use you any longer. Go and sin no more. Live a victorious life in Christ Jesus. If you make some mistakes in this area again, don't give up. We'll all be attacked by this King Saul spirit again and again. Repent and confess, pray the prayer again and just keep on going forward, until you are in total victory over it. You can overcome this spirit, never forget that.

CHAPTER 4

A Word to the Pastors

—⁓—

Pastor, I don't want to tell you what to do with such a situation; you're the leader and you've got a lot of experience. However, I can tell you this! If the King Saul spirit has showed up in your church and you've tried to work out the situation, gently and in love, and nothing works, you'll have to try a different approach. Maybe you've spoken to the person being attacked; you've counseled them and asked them to stop doing what they're doing, but they don't. You've prayed with them and prayed for them for the last six months, but nothing's changed. Sir, there might come a time when you'll have to address this issue the harder way. You will have to ask this person to leave the church and join another church. In other words, let them go or let them resign, which-ever way. They don't need to be allowed to destroy your church and your people. I can just hear some of you saying, *"That's insensitive; that's not love."* No, it's not being insensitive. If you don't let them go, they'll destroy you, your church, and their own lives, too. It's better for their sake that they leave the church; your church has a better chance of surviving and growing without them. Jesus loved the people, but He drove the troublemakers out of the church with a whip, remember?

> And He found in the temple those who sold oxen and sheep and doves, and the moneychangers doing business. When <u>He had made a whip</u> of cords, <u>He drove them all out of the temple</u>, with the sheep and the oxen, and poured out the changers' money and overturned the tables. And He said to those who sold doves, "Take these things away! Do not make My Father's house a house of merchandise!"
>
> —John 2:14-16, (emphasis mine)

I'm not saying use a whip to get rid of them, but you know what I mean. I've seen and heard of pastors who did not identify this King Saul spirit; they tried everything and nothing changed. They never gave up; they walked in love, prayed, fasted, and did all they could, but never took the final step of counterattacking this King Saul spirit. It destroyed their churches and a lot of their members, too. You'll have to stop it in its tracks or you'll have problems for a very long time . . . until you have a split in your church. Then it's too late. I hope you'll take some good advice today, because I've seen the destruction that this spirit has caused, all over the country.

I've seen a lot of churches split. I've seen a lot of Christians backslide because of this spirit. Please don't allow it to destroy you and your church.

I pray that God will help you, giving you the wisdom and knowledge to handle this King Saul spirit. Every situation is different. So ask God for help and discernment, with your church's situation. I pray that your church will stay healthy and that the members of your church will not allow the King Saul spirit to use them. I pray that you and your church will be blessed. Let's get this King Saul spirit out of our churches and overcome the enemy. **1 John 4:4** says, *"You are of God, little children, and have <u>overcome them</u>, because <u>He who is in you is greater than he who is in the world</u>"* (emphasis mine). The "them" in this verse can be translated as the King Saul spirit. It can be overcome by the power of God that is in us. We have to get to the point where we realize we have power over it, and it has no power over us. We are the overcomers.

CONCLUSION

—ᴡᴡ—

Remember the story of Rob, the upcoming worship leader? If only he had adapted the King David spirit. If only he had truly repented and turned away from his sin, rather than destroying Brother Thomas and splitting up his church. If Rob had only realized that God would have restored the whole situation, perhaps he still could have become the new worship leader. He didn't do that, and as we know, today Rob's back in the world, backslidden. Rob needed an encounter with God like Paul had. If only Rob had walked back into the light of God and acted as a light, rather than put out the light. Rob should have become blind to the characteristics of the King Saul spirit. He should have asked God what to do and not taken matters into his own hands, reacting in the flesh.

Poor Rob, he should have listened to his pastor and God's Word. He should have made right with God, but Rob's relationship with God just got worse. Rob could have let the pastor and the elders pray for him and deliver him from this King Saul spirit. He never allowed anyone to try and help him and never accepted their advice. Rob was too prideful, and the fall followed soon thereafter. Rob was never prepared to change his way of life, like Paul did, or his way of thinking. Rob chose to listen to the King Saul spirit instead. He destroyed himself, along with many of his fellow brothers and sisters in Christ. He also split up the church. Now, none of these people are in church. Rob's not even singing anymore. The anointing on his life has departed. Rob committed spiritual suicide and destroyed everything that God had given him. All of this happened because Rob chose to allow the King Saul spirit to attack, control, and use him. He killed the wrong people. He should have killed the King Saul spirit, but instead, he became a product of the King Saul spirit.

What about you and me? Are we just another Rob, who will spiritually die someday, or are we going to be like King David and the Apostle Paul, who overcame this King Saul spirit? Are we going to wake up and discern who this spirit is and what it's doing in our lives and in our churches? Are we going to make use of the Word of God, the blood of Jesus, the name of Jesus, the angels, and the Holy Spirit to counterattack the King Saul spirit? Are we going to put on the armor of God to protect us against this evil spirit? Or are we just going to be another church, splitting up, losing our members forever, and risking spiritual suicide? It's our own choice, a choice we have to make. No one can do it for us. Well, I know what I'm going to do, and if you want to join me, you're welcome. So let's get out there and let's stop this spirit.

Kill the King Saul spirit before it kills ya'll's spirit.

RECEIVING JESUS AS YOUR SAVIOR AND YOUR HEALER

—ʍ—

Choosing to receive Jesus Christ as your Savior and your Healer is the greatest miracle that can ever happen to you. It will be the most important decision you'll ever make!

If this is your first time, or if it is a recommitment, the Word of God promises in **Romans 10:9-10** *"that if you confess with your mouth the Lord Jesus and believe in your heart that God has raised Him from the dead, you will be saved. For with the heart one believes unto righteousness, and with the mouth confession is made unto salvation."* **Romans 10:13** says, *"For whoever calls on the name of the Lord shall be saved."*

God has done all He can do for your salvation and your healing. He sent Jesus, His only Son, to die for all your sins; all you have to do is believe and receive.

Pray this prayer out loud: *"Father, I confess and repent of all of my sins. Thank You for sending Jesus to die on the cross for all my sins and sickness. I confess and believe that He died, He rose from the dead, and He is sitting at the right hand of God. Thank You for forgiving and healing me. Come into my heart, Lord Jesus, and be my Lord, my Savior, and my Healer. Change me from the old man, to a new man. Deliver me Lord from every curse, bondage and every addiction in my life. By faith in Your Word, I now receive my salvation my healing and my deliverance. I am now a child of God, born again in my spirit, and You are my Father. Thank You for saving, healing and delivering me Lord, in the name of Jesus Christ, amen."*

Now you are a brand new person in Christ. Your old life is in the past. It's gone; it's over, forgiven and forgotten by God. So you have to let go of it, too. Your new life is in Christ Jesus. Get into a good Bible-teaching, faith-believing church, and serve God with your whole heart. Make sure to read the Word and pray continually. Congratulations, you are now a born-again child of God.

RECEIVING THE HOLY SPIRIT

—ɯ—

Now that you are born-again, God wants to give you His supernatural power to be able to live this new life. He wants to baptize you with the Holy Spirit. *"If you then, being evil, know how to give good gifts to your children, how much more will your heavenly Father give the Holy Spirit to those who ask Him!"* (**Luke 11:13**). You need to be baptized with the Holy Spirit. This power of God will change your life even more. To be able to receive this baptism of the Holy Spirit, all you have to do is ask, believe, and receive.

> *"Father, I thank You for saving me, healing me and delivering me. I recognize my need to have Your power to live my Christian life. I ask You to baptize me with the Holy Ghost, right now. Fill me with power from on high, so I can be a witness for You. Fill me with Your Holy Spirit, Lord. I believe and receive it right now, by faith. Thank You, Lord. I'm*

baptized with the Holy Spirit. I welcome You Holy Spirit, into my life, Amen."

I congratulate you; you are now full of the supernatural power of the Holy Spirit. You will be hearing some syllables from a heavenly language you don't know. Go ahead and speak these words out loud by faith. You will be releasing God's power from within and building yourself up in the spirit as well (**1 Cor. 14:2, 4, 14**).

ABOUT THE AUTHOR

—ᴍ—

Hansie Steyn is the founder and president of Hansie Steyn Ministries, Inc. Originally from South Africa, this evangelist and singer currently travels all over America with his family, ministering the Word of God in conferences, revival meetings, live preaching, music broadcasts, and church services. The rich heritage and accent from the nation of South Africa permeates this family's ministry of teaching God's Word, singing Holy Spirit-inspired original songs, prophetic utterances, and praying for the sick. Salvations, signs, wonders, deliverances, miracles, and healings are a part of the Steyns' meetings. Hansie, his wife Jeanette, and their daughter Elizabeth are now living in America.

To contact Hansie Steyn, please email or call:
Hansie Steyn Ministries, Inc.
E-mail them at: hsteyn1@aol.com
Visit them on the web at: www.hansiesteyn.org
Call them for prayer or bookings at: 903-681-2794

Printed in the United States
214845BV00001B/2/P